THE OPTIMIZER

NEW DEGREE PRESS

THE OPTIMIZER

Building and Leading a Team of Serial Innovators

ISBN	978-1-63676-573-0	*Paperback*
	978-1-63676-176-3	*Kindle Ebook*
	978-1-63676-177-0	*Ebook*

"The greatest danger in times of turbulence is not the turbulence – it is to act with yesterday's logic."

– PETER DRUCKER

CONTENTS

INTRODUCTION

───────

At 1:00 a.m. on March 12, 2000, I stood in the middle of a dimly lit seven-thousand-square-foot warehouse event venue on Houston Street in New York City, surrounded by about one thousand people and thumping bass. Clusters of dangling blue and red bulbs lit the space, their light diffused by sheer drapes hung between evenly spaced load-bearing iron columns to form outer rooms and a central dance floor. The red bulbs hovered over the bar in front of mirrors, expanding their glow. Twenty-two cases of liquor from the title sponsor, Jameson Irish Whisky, were stacked behind the bar. This was the annual marquee event party for the New York Underground Film Festival (NYUFF), capping off five nights of showcasing dozens of independent films and parties.

As I walked through the crowd to check in with the event staff, I stopped to speak with guests and carefully avoided bumping into an aspiring actor who had painted his entire body silver, from head to toe. As I side-stepped this "Silver-man" to avoid the paint, I couldn't help but wonder what a young Wall Street guy was doing at this party. I wasn't the only one surprised by my presence.

I approached a group of friends sitting in a circle of chairs and asked, "How's it going?"

The one unknown person in the group replied, "Leave us alone, dork."

"That guy put this entire event together," my friend sitting next to him quickly pointed out.

How did a young Wall Street person working for an asset manager come to be involved with an independent film festival?

My firm had rejected me for several promotions. I asked for a meeting with a potential new boss, Michael Keogh, who was something of a mentor but had turned down my last promotion request. He shared some solid advice.

"You need to have a more well-rounded skillset to work on my team."

I asked, "How do I do that without an opportunity to prove myself?"

He suggested I find volunteer work outside the firm to expand my skills.

I set out to find that work, and soon met Ed Halter, the director of the NYUFF. We chatted about the event and I asked, "How do you find your sponsors?"

"We could use some help, as a few sponsors have dropped off," he replied.

We agreed to a commission-only pay structure, and from that day forward, I spent many of my nights and weekends seeking sponsors.

My first idea was to see who ran ads in the *Village Voice*, a local paper, and who ran them in an East Village independent film rental store. From there I created a target list and began reaching out. I knew NYUFF needed a new liquor sponsor, so I initially focused my energy there. After limited results from calling company advertising and marketing departments, I learned I was targeting the right companies but asking the wrong questions.

When I was finally able to speak on the phone with someone from Jameson Irish Whiskey, I asked, "How do sponsorship deals happen?"

"We let our PR team lead that," she replied.

I asked, "Can I get a contact there?"

She shared her PR contact, and after several meetings, they agreed to be the first ever NYUFF title sponsor for twenty-five thousand dollars and to supply twenty-two cases of whiskey for the parties.

I didn't set out to be a Director of Sponsorship for a film festival and build a small army to plan and design six nights of parties; I was just trying to expand my skillset. The experience of hitting roadblocks, learning, and trying a new approach was invaluable.

Nine months later, I applied for a position on Michael Keogh's team again. This time I landed the promotion and my career took off. After a few more promotions and relocations, I landed a Senior Vice President leadership role managing a sales team with an annual goal of four billion dollars. Sometimes people need to get outside of their comfort zone to grow, and learning is always critical. Spending time with the creative souls in the independent film world proved to be a perfect catalyst for my growth.

THE HITS KEEP COMING

Another example of getting outside of your comfort zone to learn and iteratively grow is Amazon and Mechanical Turk (MTurk). They didn't set out to create a new business, much less a global crowd-sourcing marketplace for simple Human Intelligence Tasks (HITs) when they launched MTurk in 2005.[1] Amazon faced the problem of managing tens of thousands of duplicate products appearing on their website as their offerings radically expanded from books to virtually everything, and it simply had to be overcome.[2]

---

1   Oscar Schwartz, "Untold History of AI: How Amazon's Mechanical Turkers Got Squeezed Inside the Machine," *IEEE Spectrum*, April 22, 2019.

2   Ibid.

After several unsuccessful attempts by Amazon engineers to find a technology solution, a certain employee thought differently. Venky Harinarayan, a general manager (GM), found a solution by shifting away from the comfort of technology to which Amazon was so accustomed.[3] He wanted to get people involved.

His idea was to divide the tasks into subtasks and outsource them to humans with a computer, anywhere in the world, to complete the project. After failed attempts with a technology fix, Harinarayan realized that unlike a computer, a human can quickly look at two product descriptions and see that they are the same. Thus, MTurk was born.[4] This was a good fit, as hiring the huge workforce to make the problem go away created more challenges, and with a globally connected world, they could source workers from anywhere and keep costs low.

Amazon quickly found solid results by outsourcing this challenge in small segments to workers around the world, and their website problem soon was a relic. Later in 2005, seeing the success of solving this problem with a human solution, Jeff Bezos, Amazon's CEO, recognized the opportunity to offer this service to anyone who wanted a micro task done and opened it to all.[5]

---

3   Ibid.

4   Ibid.

5   Ibid.

Today, MTurk acts as a hub connecting a global workforce and companies in need of solving simple tasks. The company gets a low-cost solution, the employee gets paid a wage and Amazon collects a fee. The worker base is over 250,000 and operates across dozens of countries.[6] Any company needing help with a micro task can submit it through MTurk, and any MTurk worker can bid on the project.

Amazon borrowed the Mechanical Turk name from a supposed Artificial Intelligence robotic chess master built in the 1770s by inventor Wolfgang von Kempelen.[7] The MTurk defeated dignitaries such as Benjamin Franklin and Napoléon but turned out to have a human hiding inside of it who was secretly making the chess moves, which made it a perfect name for Amazon's new tool. MTurk runs thousands of HITs per day with the cost and scale of software but ironically has humans conducting the tasks, not machines, just like the Mechanical Turk from the 1770s.[8]

I wanted to see if the iterative approach of making several different attempts to solve the Amazon duplicate product listing issue that spawned MTurk was unique or really part of a larger trend. What I discovered changed the way I see innovation today.

---

6   Jonathan Robinson et al., "Tapped Out or Barely Tapped? Recommendations for How to Harness the Vast and Largely Unused Potential of the Mechanical Turk Participant Pool," *Plos One*, (December 16, 2019): 3.

7   Schwartz, "Untold."

8   Ibid.

IT'S A JOURNEY, NOT A DESTINATION

Innovation is a journey of learning. As you work through several attempts to solve for a current need and refine your approach at each step, ultimately you move closer to the solution. This is optimizing. I experienced this with the multi-step approach to landing the title sponsor for NYUFF and with the example of MTurk. This concept isn't limited to technology companies; it spans the universe of industries. You must approach this journey with eyes wide open and recognize there will be challenges and risks along the way.

Optimization is about consistently solving problems that create value for your customers and business. Far more than thriving for many years, it's about staying relevant in your field as change is constantly knocking at your door. When change knocks, you must answer. Not everyone is ready for that. This is evidenced by research from Innosight, an innovation consultancy, and the historical turnover in the Standard & Poor's 500 (S&P 500) stock index members. If your company was listed on the S&P 500 in 1964, you stayed on that list for an average of 33 years.[9]

Innosight predicts that by 2027, the average S&P 500 tenure will drop by 64 percent, down to twelve years.[10] If companies continue operating entirely as they did twelve years ago, they will rapidly approach irrelevance. Or, they are well on their way to trouble and no one has noticed or been brave

---

9   Scott D. Anthony et al., "2018 Corporate Longevity Forecast: Creative Destruction is Accelerating," *Innosight*, February 2018.

10 Ibid.

enough to speak up. Look no further than Macy's, an iconic US retailer that was demoted on March 31, 2020 from the S&P 500 large cap index to the S&P 600 small cap index (less than $1.4 billion market cap) due to its dramatic decline in stock price.[11] Contrast the outcome of this 162-year-old retailer to that of Amazon that launched in 1994 and now has the second largest stock valuation in the world.[12] Amazon used serial optimization to achieve world class success, while Macy's has lost its relevance, and its success has deflated.

In my own career working for a large asset manager, I often found myself frustrated by the apathy many had toward innovation or optimization. My firm spent years trying to move a seasoned sales force from heavy briefcases stuffed with high-cost literature to iPads with digital delivery, but that journey was never entirely fulfilled. New ideas are rarely the issue. For change to take place, issues must be recognizable, actions executable, and employee engagement improved. More importantly, it must be clear to those impacted by the change that the gain of adoption will outweigh the pain it brings.

Unfortunately, history has proved that change often means lower wages, more work, or, worse yet, job loss. My father's employer of thirty years, A.C. Nielsen, was acquired by a competitor in 1987. The acquisition was predictably framed

---

11 Claudia Assis, "Macy's to leave the S&P 500 index," *MarketWatch*, March 31, 2020.

12 "20 Largest Companies by Market Capitalization," *The Online Investor*, update September 13, 2020.

as an opportunity for business growth. Within two years, he was forced into early retirement at age fifty-seven along with several coworkers. This taught me a powerful lesson early on that you're never secure in your role. You have to grow.

Change in companies is often ambiguous as to who will benefit, making many employees incredibly anxious along the way. It is not surprising that when many people hear the word innovation, their minds jump to radical change which is rarely in their favor. Depending on their level of trust in their managers and willingness to attempt something new, they often have a fight-or-flight response.

I believe innovation doesn't create radical change in the short term. Innovation is incremental, and this transformation is more powerful when it happens over time. An outsider who merely witnesses the beginning and end point sees enormous innovation, but they miss the long journey of learning through a series of optimizations to solve a real problem. Companies generally don't solve problems on the first attempt; they see failures along the way. The benefit to incremental change is not only driving results but reducing the emotional drain on your team associated with evolving.

I feel compelled to write this story because I've seen so many people over two decades who had the power to make their business grow but never found a way to effectively unleash that gift and pull the company forward, either through themselves or with the help of a great leader.

While hosting my first team meeting as a new sales leader for a large New York–based asset management firm, I explained that constant improvement would be a crucial part of our journey together in building a business. I asked an open-ended question to share my vision:

"How are we all going to grow more efficient and effective in what we do on a consistent basis?"

The rolling of eyes around the room was dizzying and told me this wasn't going to be a quick solve. After the meeting ended, a senior member of the team pulled me aside and asked:

"How are we going to get better all the time?"

"Together, day by day," I replied.

In the following months, I spent many hours getting to know my team members and developing a relationship with each person. As trust grew, positive, incremental change began to take hold across the team and became contagious. Soon the team members were pulling each other along and raising the standard for all. This validated the power of trust to enable anyone on a team to try to think differently, ask deeper questions about their business, and take calculated risks. We'll explore several examples of these changes later.

Each team member doesn't grow at the same pace, but with motivation that makes them feel safe, they can all elevate what they bring to the table. I call this "lifting the curve," as in lifting the talent bell curve for a team. Everyone is initially ranked differently in terms of what they offer, but they can all grow more innovative and bring new, quality ideas to the team. A significant part of this lift is giving people a sense of ownership and leadership opportunities. They have to know this is their business and focus on straightforward questions:

How can you help to improve our business? How can we utilize your learning and help the team rise with you?

Each person on my team had some level of creativity. However, two perennial top performers on the team, Rick and Josh, were consistently innovative in their thinking and were never afraid to fail. More importantly, their mindset was geared toward deeply knowing their best clients and effectively optimizing existing resources to better relate to their audience, ultimately growing their sales.

After discussing an opportunity for them to teach peers a new strategy for leveraging the skills they'd developed, Rick and Josh felt not only challenged but also highly empowered. They embraced the exercise and dove straight into planning mode with me. Their work finally delivered the training lift I needed and gave them a valuable opportunity to reflect on what they'd done and how they did it so they could effectively teach it to their peers. We'll explore this example in greater detail later.

The key lesson is Optimize to Innovate; understanding the power of iteration, incremental change, and empowerment in driving change within organizations is paramount to success. You can't do this alone. You must allow your team to take risks, with their leader playing an active role in letting them know they're in a safe place.

Ironically, I never specifically used the word "optimization" until I began to do research for this book and finally found a name for how I've thought for years.

This book will provide valuable leadership lessons through examples, such as: pull (don't push) your team forward; enable your team to drive change through becoming a trusted advisor; empower your team to think differently by letting them lead. Read on so that you too can Lift the Curve and sustain a culture of optimization. First, let's look at how we landed here by exploring the history of innovation.

PART 1

HOW WE
GOT HERE

CHAPTER 1

INNOVATION IS OPTIMIZATION

———

Every radio station was barking in unison on Friday, August 13, 2004, in my new hometown of Orlando, Florida. The sky was blanketed with light-gray, puffy clouds: a hurricane. This storm was predicted to be the worst ever to hit central Florida with winds up to 150 miles per hour. Disney World and Universal Studios closed their gates. Traffic was crawling as residents scurried for supplies. My phone rang. I flipped it open. It was my wife.

"Hi, Dina."

"I'm at the store. It's a mess. There's no bottled water or canned food! We also need candles!"

"Candles?" I replied.

"Yes, get candles too!"

The storm rolled through and we didn't have power for three sweaty days of books by candlelight. We don't spend much time pondering the light bulb, until our only options are candles or a flashlight.

THEN THERE WAS LIGHT

The first electric lamp was created in 1802 by the English serial inventor Humphry Davy.[13] Davy improved upon Alessandro Volta's work of generating electricity and solved a perennial problem, escaping darkness at will.[14] The charm of candlelight has appeal, but as the sole source of illumination, it hardly compares to electric lighting.

The world was in wonder of Davy's new light, but it was incredibly bright and burned out quickly.[15] People needed a better solution. Dozens of scientists made thousands of attempts, and seventy-seven years later, the light bulb was commercially viable and patented in the first known Research and Development (R&D) lab, built by Thomas Edison, the father of modern innovation.[16] Edison didn't invent the light bulb; rather, through thousands of attempts with his team, he made it accessible to anyone with one dollar.[17]

13   Elizabeth Palmero, "Who Invented the Light Bulb?" *Live Science*, August 17, 2017.

14   Ibid.

15   Ibid.

16   Ibid.

17   "How Much Did the First Light Bulb Cost?" *Reference*, March 25, 2020.

"Edison's genius was improving on others' technologies and making them more practical for the general public," Historian Patrick Kiger shared.[18] His most important innovation, however, was the process of modern invention itself.[19] Inside his R&D invention lab in Menlo Park, New Jersey, he was the first to apply the principles of mass production to the solitary inventor model by bringing scientists, machinists, and designers together to work side by side.[20] This groundbreaking model got all of these skills working together in one building, generally with the purpose of improving upon existing ideas.

> *Edison's superpower was to see failure as a learning opportunity and to push onward.*

As he once shared, "I have not failed. I've just found ten thousand ways that won't work."[21] We don't often appreciate Edison's relentless love affair with problems until we experience a black out. Edison understood that he needed a team to work through this critical process of learning and thousands of steps to get to the answer. And, we must not overlook his ability to work behind the scenes, enabling and

---

18 Patrick Kiger, "6 Key Inventions by Thomas Edison," *History*, March 6 ,2020.

19 "Thomas Edison and Menlo Park," Menlo Park Museum, accessed July 13, 2020.

20 Ibid.

21 "Thomas Edison Quotes," *Good Reads*, accessed July 13, 2020.

inspiring a small army to always push forward, time after time. During your next frustrating power outage, ponder Edison's ten thousand attempts!

Thomas Edison inherited his entrepreneurial spirit from his father, and he inherited his world view from his mother, a teacher, who taught him to "read good books, quickly and correctly."[22] During his career he founded fourteen companies, including the predecessor to General Electric and patented 1,093 inventions.[23] When he passed away in 1931, the *New York Times* estimated the value of the industries based on his inventions at fifteen billion dollars.[24] In 2020, the value of this would be $393 billion.[25] This is wealth creation through optimization at its best.

Edison never quit learning or asking larger questions, nor did he come up with new ideas in a vacuum. He constantly evolved his work through numerous attempts until he found true value. He had a strong business sense from his father to understand if he was going to commit the time to make something, it had to be something people wanted.[26] He didn't set out to make a better candle. Edison's vision was much

---

22 "Want to Save The World? Start Thinking Like Thomas Edison," *Real Leaders*, October 17, 2015.

23 "Thomas Edison Center | Menlo Park Museum."

24 "Want to Save The World?"

25 "Inflation Calculator | Find US Dollar's Value from 1913-2020," accessed September 15, 2020.

26 "Want to Save The World?"

larger. He sought to illuminate the world and was willing to put in the work to make it a reality.[27]

NECESSITY IS THE MOTHER OF INVENTION

What is innovation? How does it happen? Rather than sorting through 1.5 billion hits on Google for innovation, let's look at the official *Merriam-Webster* dictionary definition. According to *Webster's*, innovation can refer to something new or to a change made to an existing product, idea, or field. The telephone was an invention, the smartphone an innovation.[28]

> *History has shown us that innovation rarely changes the world on its first try, and falling in love with your solution for the world rather than solving a real problem is a fast track to the trash bin.*

"Fall in love with the problem, not the solution"

−URI LEVINE, WAZE COFOUNDER

Mankind has been inventing new ideas since day one for a vast number of reasons and has created enormous economic gains. The great philosopher Plato said that "necessity is the

---

27 Ibid.

28 *Merriam-Webster*, s.v. "innovation," accessed July 12, 2020.

mother of invention."[29] We needed fire to keep warm and cook food, the printing press to share the written word, vehicles to quickly transport us and move goods, and iPhone photo filters to make selfies post-worthy.

However, when new ideas come along, they're often born somewhat ugly and need refinement. This is where blood, sweat, tears, and collaboration come in. History and the present are overflowing with creative thinking and new product ideas, but the most well-known stories are rarely focused on the original idea. History often recognizes the outcome of many iterations and optimizations that solve meaningful problems.

> *People don't remember the person with the idea, they remember the person who made it highly useful.*

THE DATA DILEMMA

Looking over my career on Wall Street, I found the iteration concept highly effective. In 2014, as a new manager and a believer in leveraging data, I was asked to lead the sales data delivery and consumption efforts. We were investing heavily in data and a return on investment was necessary. In researching the current methods, I found there was no standardization for effectively leveraging data by leaders or

---

29   Gary Martin, "Necessity is the mother of invention," *The Phrase Finder*, accessed July 6, 2020.

their sales teams. Many found their own way and some simply opted out from frustration.

Sitting with my data analyst, Sheetal, we focused on the problem and asked, "How can we present the most relevant data so the sales force can easily target their best sales opportunities?" We knew if we could simplify the use of data for the sales team, it would drive usage and help the team be far more targeted and impactful in their marketing strategies.

Where Do You Start?
We solicited a diverse list of names from other sales managers to develop a pilot group to help build new data dashboards. We wanted a range of skill sets to ensure we helped the widest audience. We surveyed the group to better understand how to deliver value in the data and make it easily consumable. With these insights and our own analysis, we built a beta version of the dashboard.

We brought the dashboard back to the pilot group to test its efficacy and learned even more. No one wanted to spend hours mining, nor should they. The key points needed to be clear and give direction toward achieving goals. We tweaked the dashboard once again and then released it to a broader audience. We asked for one last round of feedback and soon opened the dashboard to all. Going forward, we only needed to make marginal changes.

This iteration delivered greater efficiency in business planning for the salesforce and helped the organization see more clearly why and where we needed to change our product focus. It helped build a strong case for leading our larger business strategy and was done with existing resources and people. Lastly, with so many involved in the process, it was easier to grow adoption of these reports once they rolled out, as we had dozens of existing advocates that saw the power of the new reporting.

As the value grew from the data, we upgraded from Microsoft Excel to a leading data visualization software program and repeated the pilot process. The outcome formed the basis for how data is consumed today by that sales force. It made the sales team more efficient and it helped the firm make better decisions for future initiatives. This simplified reporting helped my team grow their focus on a new suite of Exchange Traded Funds (ETF) we launched. We built the largest ETF asset base in the firm at over $650 million.

A LOOK BACK: FROM TRACTORS TO TESLA

To gain some greater historical perspective on innovation, I sought the insights of Robert Atkinson, the president and founder of the Information Technology and Innovation Foundation. He shared with me that he has "never seen a new product that got it exactly right on the first try." It's always a series of improvements.

To get a sense of where he has seen serial improvements have a major impact on an economy, he shared, "The most disruptive innovation in American History was the farming tractor," which was first seen in 1890.

"Why?" I asked.

"No other invention has dislocated the US job market more."

In the decade leading to this breakthrough invention, the US had over four million farms and a post–Civil War industrial boom.[30] These farms employed over 51 percent of all Americans that year. By 1910, when the tractor was on its way to commercial success, farm employment accounted for only 31 percent and has dropped to single digits since.[31] We still need food but have radically expanded output per worker thanks to tractors and, therefore, need fewer people to work the fields.

Did the inventor profit from it? Have you ever heard of John Froehlich, the man credited with inventing the tractor?[32] No? How about John Deere? In 1890, looking for a way to harvest grain more safely and efficiently, Froehlich worked with a blacksmith to create the first tractor powered by a gasoline engine.[33] He later joined forces with Waterloo Gasoline Engine Company in 1895 but left after one year after only two units were sold.[34] Waterloo saw the opportunity

---

30 US Census Bureau, "Eleventh Census - Volume 5. Statistics of Agriculture in the US," The United States Census Bureau, accessed September 15, 2020.

31 Conference on Research in Income and Wealth, National Bureau of Economic Research, and Economic History Association (U.S.), *Output, Employment, and Productivity in the United States after 1800*. (New York: National Bureau of Economic Research; distributed by Columbia University Press, 1966).

32 History com Editors, "John Froelich, Inventor of the Gas-Powered Tractor, Is Born," *History*, accessed September 15, 2020.

33 Ibid.

34 Ibid.

of the tractor and focused on their legacy business, engine sales, to stay afloat as they continued to refine the tractor.[35]

In 1913, they finally had a commercially viable version and sales saw a marginal lift. They continued to improve the machine and sold 118 units in 1914.[36] By 1917, World War I was well underway, and with the US entering the war, demand took off for heavy machinery to supply the war effort.[37] During these years, they continued allocating resources to improving the tractor. Clearly, their method of iteration wasn't delivering the desired results quickly enough. There was a missing link.

Nothing Runs like a Deere

John Deere found his start after moving his young family from his home state of Vermont to seek better opportunities in Illinois.[38] He quickly found work in a blacksmith shop and found project inspiration while listening to farmers' equipment concerns. The current wooden plows were made for the sandy soil in the eastern US, and Deere soon learned they were not effective in cutting the thick midwestern prairie soil.[39]

---

35 Ibid.

36 Ibid.

37 "Lessons in the How: Deere Visits Henry Ford," *The John Deere Journal*, August 13, 2018.

38 "Past Leaders," John Deere Corporation, accessed July 8, 2020.

39 Jackson Landers, "Did John Deere's Best Invention Spark a Revolution or an Environmental Disaster?" *Smithsonian Magazine*, accessed September 14, 2020.

After many attempts, he invented his first plow in 1837 to solve the soil problem.[40] The keys to his new plow were a stronger material (steel) and making it highly polished and properly shaped to better cut furrows and not let dirt stick to itself.[41] He then tested his new plow on different soil types to ensure it would work.[42] It did.

In 1918, Deere, this serial optimizer and now successful plow manufacturer, saw an opportunity for growth. He purchased Waterloo tractors as a better way to pull his plows through the fields, rather than horses. Deere paid $2.1 million ($34.8 million in 2018 dollars) for this acquisition.[43] This was a solid match. Waterloo was known for continuously improving engines and John Deere for plows, but Deere had stronger financial resources.

With Waterloo on board, John Deere now had a viable product that the market demanded. A highly efficient plowing machine that didn't need water breaks. They sold 5,634 units in their first year together.[44]

The tractor increased farm production by four times compared to work done by a horse and farmhand.[45] Despite

---

40   Ibid.

41   Ibid.

42   John Finegan, "The Steel Plow," *Iroqouis West*, accessed July 9, 2020.

43   "100 Years Since the Purchase of The Waterloo Boy," *AgWeb*, March 19, 2018.

44   Ibid.

45   Robert Atkinson, "Resistance is Futile," interview by Ramtin Arablouei and Rund Abdelfatah, *Throughline*, NPR, April 25, 2019, audio, 37:01.

this early win, John Deere has not relied on past success for growth. In addition to constantly listening to customers, truly understanding needs, and working to improve their products, they've consistently delivered to make farmers more productive. To ensure this effort, they borrowed the R&D lab idea from Thomas Edison and built the John Deere Technology Innovation Center in partnership with the University of Illinois Urbana-Champaign.[46]

One result of their relentless innovation focus was in 2020. Deere was honored at the Consumer Electronics Show (CES) in the "Better World" category for a new tractor that integrates artificial intelligence, the internet, and advanced automation.[47] They set out to make tractors easier to use and to better optimize their impact on the land, thus improving sustainability.[48] Their iterative approach to advancing the tractors' capabilities has driven efficiency and helped the environment.

Deere is now the largest tractor manufacturer in the world valued at almost sixty billion dollars.[49] They never stop the improvement journey. Innovation and optimization are not destinations; they are part of a never-ending process to grow

---

46 "John Deere Technology Innovation Center," University of Illinois Urbana-Champaign, accessed August 16, 2020.

47 "John Deere 8RX Tractor," Consumer Electronics Show, accessed August 15, 2020.

48 Ibid.

49 Sweta Killa, "John Deere Q2 Results Put Agribusiness ETFs in Focus," *Yahoo Finance*, May 26, 2020.

and stay highly relevant to your customers. Few know that better than Deere.

Have we seen similar examples in modern times where a new technology came along and someone else improved upon it to change the world?

Money, Motors, and Mars

Tesla has parallels to the tractor story. Like John Deere and the tractor, Elon Musk did not invent the electric car, but he made it much, much better. The first electric car was invented in 1832 by Robert Anderson, but we'll focus on a more modern option, the GM EV1.[50] GM did market research to learn that there was strong demand for an electric car, and they set out to bring a version to mass market in 1996.[51] It quickly developed a loyal following, but it was riddled with limitations.

Beyond the interest in an electric car, GM missed the mark with product features and design. The EV1 was small with a particularly unattractive shape (for low drag) and used a lead acid battery which limited the range to under 90 miles and took up to 14 hours to charge.[52]

---

50 "Timeline: History of the Electric Car," U.S. Department of Energy, accessed August 15, 2020.

51 Eric Reed, "History of Tesla: Timeline and Facts," *The Street*, February 4, 2020.

52 Barry Winfield, "Tested: 1997 General Motors EV1 Proves to Be the Start of Something Big," Car and Driver, March 1997.

They buried this project in 2003 due to abysmal sales, and some customers literally held funerals for the EV1.[53] We know there was not just demand but a growing auto consumer segment that was emotionally connected to the idea of an electric car. This is a classic example of focusing on a chosen solution, in this case a low-cost electric car, rather than the customer problem that was identified through market research. Customers wanted a zero-emission vehicle but wanted little or no compromise from a gasoline-fueled car.

Enter Tesla, a fledgling company founded in 2003 by engineers Martin Eberhard and Marc Tarpenning in San Carlos, California. They set out to benefit from General Motors' favorable test market results for an electric car but with a better product.[54] Tesla focused on the market problem, not the electric car they wanted to bring to market.

A year into starting Tesla, Eberhard and Tarpenning were introduced to a charismatic and recently minted Silicon Valley millionaire, Elon Musk, PayPal co-founder.[55] Musk was trying to create his own electric car, the tZero, but needed help with design issues and was also busy trying to get

---

53   Aaron Brown, "Here's the Story Behind GM's Revolutionary Electric Car from the 90s That Disappeared," *Business Insider*, March 16, 2016.

54   Eric Reed, "History of Tesla: Timeline and Facts," *The Street*, February 4, 2020.

55   Taylor Locke, "Elon Musk: 'I Really Didn't Want to Be CEO of Tesla'— Here's How He Says It Happened," *CNBC*, Updated May 5, 2020.

SpaceX off the ground.[56] They decided to join forces, and Musk invested $6.3 million in Tesla.[57]

Bringing a totally new car to market was a high-risk venture, as GM learned. The most recent car company to bring something totally different to market was the failed DeLorean in 1981.[58] This history did not deter Tesla from moving forward. They had a much larger mission: accelerate the transition to sustainable energy as opposed to simply building a better electric car.[59]

Eberhard and Tarpenning didn't even set out to invent a world changing electric car. When asked in 2019 about his views on Tesla, Eberhard said: "I didn't start as an electric car enthusiast but as a non-fossil fuel enthusiast."[60] What they confirmed in the discovery process was that luxury car buyers wanted to reduce their carbon footprint. However, they wanted to do so fashionably with a driving range they were accustomed to, roughly 250 miles.[61] The ninety miles of the EV1 was not enough.

---

56   Joshua Davis, "How Elon Musk Turned Tesla into the Car Company of the Future," *Wired*, September 27, 2010.

57   Ibid.

58   Matt Blitz, "Inside the Car Company That's Resurrecting the DeLorean," *Popular Mechanics*, January 18, 2019.

59   "Tesla's mission is to accelerate the world's transition to sustainable energy," Tesla Corporation, accessed August 17, 2020.

60   Economic Times Bureau, "Martin Eberhard Calls Tesla His 'Baby,' Talks About Being Ousted from Company's Board," *The Economic Times*, updated March 1, 2019.

61   Reed, "History of Tesla."

Tesla created four versions of the original $100,000 Roadster by 2008 but gave up, focusing on the lower cost Model S.[62] The Great Recession was in full force and they needed money. The Roadster had a decent driving range, but the price tag and the 24–48 hours for charging weren't feasible to gain enough sales volume, and it came in well over estimated production cost.[63] They had a fantastic product but couldn't get cost and pricing properly aligned.

Musk took over as CEO at this point and conducted a major restructuring of the work force and finances of the company, including firing former CEO and co-founder Eberhard. He created a strategic partnership with Daimler and secured a $465 million loan from the US government.[64] They were solving the right problem just not quickly enough to generate meaningful sales.

From here, they reset their strategy. They still wanted to bring a high margin luxury car to market and did so with the Model S at $75,000 in 2012 and the Model X in 2015 at a slightly higher starting point.[65] In addition to building the Tesla Gigafactory to make lithium batteries better and more affordable, Tesla also offers over-the-air software updates. This was groundbreaking.

---

62 Jay Ramey, "The first Tesla Roadster: A look back at the early adopter's electric car," *Autoweek*, November 27, 2017.

63 Reed, "History of Tesla."

64 Ibid.

65 Visual Capitalist, "The History of Tesla in 5 Minutes," January 15, 2019, video, 5:51.

The car can upgrade itself while you sleep and save you a service call. As one enthusiastic owner shared with me, "It's the only car I've ever owned that gets better the longer I own it!" Some upgrades are free, such as improved interpretation of voice commands and a clip recording for a front facing dash cam recorder whenever you honk.[66] Other upgrades are for purchase, such as extending your battery range.[67]

"Great ideas often hide behind good ideas."

-PAT SHERIDAN, CO-FOUNDER OF MODUS
CREATE, A CONSULTANCY FIRM.

Tesla didn't simply create a better electric car and a better car-buying experience, they developed systems and processes to allow for constant improvement to make their products sustainably great. They continue to grow and make seamless incremental improvements. A recent example is the thirteen iterations Tesla went through to improve the Octovalve for their Model Y in three months.[68] Former senior design engineer for Ford, Sandy Munro, said, "I couldn't get one design change in a year at Ford."[69] Tesla not only works to

---

66 "Upgrades," Tesla Corporation, accessed August 17, 2020.

67 David Ingold, "Tesla's Betting You'll Pay $9,000 for a Software Upgrade," *Bloomberg*, June 10, 2016.

68 *Tesla Daily*, "Tesla Battery Day Teaser, Extortion Sting Operation, Octovalve Updates, Lucid Air Battery," August 27, 2020, video, 11:01.

69 Ibid.

continually improve their cars; they increase their rate of change of improvement.

Consumers have rewarded Tesla's focus on excellence. All three Tesla car models (prior to the recent Model Y) have been top ten sellers of all electric vehicles.[70] Furthermore, the recent Model 3 accounted for 23 percent of all small and mid-size luxury vehicle sales in 2019.[71] Tesla has found exceptional balance between innovation and optimization while working to grow adoption of energy sustainability. This type of out-side-of-the-box thinking drives economic growth beyond the doors of a single factory.

IDEAS ARE EASY

Looking forward, according to the International Monetary Fund (IMF), global economic growth will slow, largely due to stalled international trade.[72] This does not preclude countries from continuing to grow; the IMF predicts China will maintain the top spot for contributing to global growth in 2024.[73]

---

70 Mark Kane, "Top 10 Best-Selling Plug-In Electric Cars in U.S. - 2019 Edition," *Insideevs*, January 11, 2020.

71 Zachary Shahan, "Tesla Model 3 Dominates US Premium-Class Small & Midsize Car Market — 23 percent of 2019 Sales*," Clean Tech, January 18, 2020.

72 Alexandre Tanzi, "These 20 Countries Will Dominate Global Growth in 2024," *Bloomberg*, October 19, 2019.

73 Ibid.

They will grow because they continue to make innovation a top priority for their country's recurring strategic five-year plans and have established a road map to get there.[74] India and the United States will take the next two spots, respectively, for adding to global growth, but the US contribution is trending lower.[75] Robert Atkinson told me, "The US has not put forth a national innovation strategy since the Carter administration." Capitalism has served us well, but there needs to a be a future plan with a target.

Innovation is critical to making our lives better, keeping businesses competitive, and helping economies grow. It needs to be in our blood. But innovation alone doesn't often win. Ideas are the easy part. Optimizing them into value is the challenge, as Edison, Deere, and Musk learned.

> *Innovation takes enormous energy and is often an improvement upon an existing idea through a series of iterations. Optimizing with a larger vision for growth can push creativity further. The originator of the idea rarely wins.*

Failure and learning are part of the journey to success and, therefore, need to be acceptable outcomes, and your team needs to understand this issue well.

---

74 Michael Lelyveld, "China Unveils New Strategy for Economic Growth," *Radio Free Asia*, August 21, 2020.

75 Tanzi, "These 20 Countries."

There are key principles to creating a culture of innovation through optimization. Before we discuss them, we need to better understand how this change takes place in the real world, with humans involved. Innovation is a powerful force, but it creates an equally powerful opposing force—resistance—which we'll explore next.

CHAPTER 2

RESISTANCE IS FUTILE

WHAT'S IN A NAME?

"Innovator!" the judge barked as he pounded the gavel down, "you shall be imprisoned and have your ears cut."

English minister and devout Puritan, Henry Burton, was incarcerated for being seen as an innovator against the church in 1637.[76] At the time, innovation was largely seen as pursuing practices outside of the church, leaning toward Roman idolatry such as tables, altars, robes, and bowing. Ironically, Burton was promoting conservatism but went too far in a 200-page pamphlet that he circulated in town, questioning the King's authority under god.[77] Innovation sparked fear in the power structure of England as it was

---

76 Benoit Godin, "'Meddle Not with Them That Are Given to Change': Innovation as Evil," *Project on the Intellectual History of Innovation*, Working Paper no. 6 (2010): 12-27.

77 Ibid.

seen as a gateway to "disturbing the peace" and refusing subjugation to the King.[78]

It's difficult to imagine a word that is highly relied upon for economic growth today was once so vilified.

England wasn't the only culture that feared change and loss of power. Italian leaders had a similar reaction to change, not over a person, but a product: coffee. As coffee arrived in Europe in the 1600s, it was met with extreme resistance and deemed "The Devil's Drink" by the Catholic church in an effort to the banish the beans.[79] People feared it may become a substitute for current popular beverages, and it quickly became a focal point of energized gatherings; it changed social patterns and created a new way for citizens to hear news.[80]

Control appeared to be shifting away from the church. Bishops wanted to put a stop to it and presented Pope Clement VIII with a cup of coffee, expecting his condemnation. To their surprise, he found it "so delicious" that he quickly baptized it. Shortly after, the first coffee house in Rome opened.[81] Thankfully, the Pope was willing to explore a new idea before simply condemning it.

---

78 Ibid.

79 Paul Chrystal, "A drink for the devil: 8 facts about the history of coffee," *History Extra*, May 28, 2019.

80 Ibid.

81 Gretchen Filz, "The Devil's Drink: How the Pope Cheated Hell by 'Baptizing' Coffee," *GetFed*, November 15, 2018.

Bishops protested against coffee because it was new, disruptive, and seemed to reset the power structure.

> *Change brings powerful emotional forces: fear, loss, uncertainty, and shame. No one is immune.*

In this case, leaders weren't afraid of coffee; they were afraid of the loss of power and control. Pointing fingers is easier than solving real problems.

"Blame is a way to discharge pain and discomfort."
—BRENÉ BROWN

Innovation endured a negative connotation for roughly three hundred years and was replaced by renovation, restoration, and reformation, words deemed less threatening.[82] Austrian economist Joseph A. Schumpeter recognized the power of innovation for economic growth.[83] Schumpeter, known as the "Father of Creative Destruction," is credited as one of the liberators of the word innovation through his book *Business*

---

82 Benoit Godin, "'Meddle Not with Them That Are Given to Change': Innovation as Evil," *Project on the Intellectual History of Innovation*, Working Paper no. 6 (2010): 30-32.

83 Sigurd Pacher, "Innovation and Entrepreneurship - The Austrian Economist Joseph A. Schumpeter," *Austria*, March 27, 2015.

Cycles: A Theoretical, Historical, and Statistical Analysis of the Capitalist Process, published in 1939.[84]

He stated, "Invention is the act of intellectual creativity and is without importance to economic analysis, while innovation is an economic decision: a firm applying an invention or adopting an invention."[85]

Even though "innovation" had been liberated, it still did not receive a warm welcome.[86]

EMOTIONS NEVER DIE

Fear, loss, uncertainty, and shame are the cornerstones of resistance to change for employees, which coincide with innovation.[87] Fear of disruption to your current happenstance, loss of control of your power structure, uncertainty of what's next, or shame and feeling badly for who we are can play a part in halting a change initiative.[88] These powerful forces cannot be ignored as a leader.

84 Benoit Godin, "καινοτομία: An Old Word for a New World, or, The De-Contestation of a Political and Contested Concept," *Project on the Intellectual History of Innovation*, Working Paper no. 9 (2011): 39.

85 Pacher, "Innovation and Entrepreneurship."

86 Benoit Godin, "'Innovation: The History of a Category," *Project on the Intellectual History of Innovation*, Working Paper no. 1 (2008): 35.

87 Rosabeth Moss Kanter, "Ten Reasons People Resist Change," *HBR*, September 25, 2012.

88 Guy Winch, PhD, "10 Signs That You Might Have Fear of Failure," *Psychology Today*, June 18, 2018.

Resisting change has been with us for centuries, as we saw with Mr. Burton, and history has shown us repeatedly how this cycle plays out. Fear of change can paralyze us as we ponder disruption to our lives and contemplate new responsibilities, a need for further education, a new commute, a new compensation plan, unemployment, or failure.

Change is often a story of loss, and when we lose, we grieve. The five stages of grief cannot be overlooked when navigating change because something will be gone forever.

The five stages of grief include: Denial ("I'm not doing it"), Anger ("That's a terrible idea"), Bargaining ("If we change this, can we still hold on to that?"), Depression ("Life will never be the same"), and Acceptance ("I guess I can live with this").[89] This is a natural part of change that is largely unavoidable, but it can be better navigated. As a leader, you need to first be aware that grief is a likely outcome of change, and if you let it fester without managing messaging and emotions, you will damage your team's trust in you.

Uncertainty is another powerful force. When tomorrow feels like a mystery, productivity will suffer as your team prioritizes job status protection over seeking growth—especially if they work remotely. When clarity is lacking, the void fills with speculation and rumor, making the sentiment worse yet.

In 2010, I had lunch with a former client, Guy Bassini. We reflected on the Great Recession, and he shared, "There were

---

89 David Kessler, "The Five Stages of Grief," *Grief*, accessed May 4, 2020.

two safe positions in 2008. Cash and fetal." For a real-time, visual measure of his view, we can compare the movement of the Chicago Board Options Exchange (CBOE) Volatility Index, a measure of stock market volatility and investor cash levels.

Since 1990, there have been two outsized spikes in the index that were roughly double any other: The Great Recession of 2008 and the early months of the coronavirus pandemic of 2020.[90] In both instances, investors made record-setting moves to cash. In 2008, cash assets reached $4 trillion, and in mid-May of 2020, cash levels hit a new record of $4.672 trillion, compared to a recent average of roughly $2.5 trillion.[91]

−ICI Money Market Assets ($B, LHS)   −CBOE Volatility Index (RHS)

Bloomberg LP.[92]

90   "VIX Index Charts & Data." Cboe Corporation, accessed August 17, 2020.

91   Jesse Pound, "There's nearly $5 trillion parked in money markets as many investors are still afraid of stocks," *CNBC*, June 22, 2020.

92   "Chart Comparing CBOE Volatility Index versus ICI Money Market Assets 1/5/90 to 8/14/20," *Bloomberg* August 2020.

It's no easy task to stand still when the stock market is violently swinging or when we don't know what is in store for our careers. As a leader, it is paramount to have acute awareness of this uncertainty and face it head-on. Transparency plays a critical role, but it is not always easy and often the entire story can't be shared. During these moments, well-rounded, well-informed, empathetic leaders can elevate credibility with their teams for years to come by engaging with them, not hiding from them.

Shame is a likely outcome of exploring a new and better way, and we fear it greatly.[93]

> *Shame can come from two directions. It can be internally or externally driven, but neither is easy to face.*

Internally, there is the shame of failing. You took a risk and it didn't work. Now, you will face consequences and others will know you failed.

The second form is the shame of wasting your life for years on a product, project, or process. This is about proper messaging. You felt you operated successfully for a period of time, and now your boss tells you it needs to be thrown away as it's not an effective approach.

---

93 Winch, PhD, "10 Signs."

It's a unique breed who is confident enough to admit to their friends, family, or boss that they tried something and failed or that years spent working have been for naught. As a leader, a message about the need for change is far better received when framed through external industry pressures rather than poor existing processes.

Research has found that the shame of failure is such a strong psychological threat that the motivation to avoid failure over-powers the motivation to succeed.[94] This is a key driver of mediocrity. This isn't because employees want to be average. It's because we fear the shame of failure and the potential results like missing out on a bonus, getting fired or having others learn that we don't always fulfill the perfect image we attempt to portray. We tend to project the best image of ourselves to the world.

Review a friend's social media photos and compare them to their average image you typically see. Is there a difference? Is it small? Likely not! We display a pristine image to make us feel a sense of confidence so we can take on any obstacle. If this image is ever threatened by our actions, we know shame is lurking right around the corner to remind us never to fail.

As leaders, we need to be aware that a combination of all of these feelings sits behind any change, and the more we prepare for that fact in our messaging and engagement with team members throughout a change, the more likely we will

---

94   Ibid.

gain adoption. This is one key reason why building trust is critical for you and each team member.

Trust Is the Glue

Along with shame avoidance, what further exacerbates fear, loss, and uncertainty is a lack of trust in the person we report to in our careers. In the absence of trust, we will not only resist change, but will also not develop and foster a mindset to solve problems and innovate on our own. McKinsey, a consultancy, estimates that 70 percent of change efforts fail, in large part due to employee resistance and leaders not effectively shifting mindsets and behaviors.[95] Trust issues already exist; change brings them to the front of the line.

Leaders play a significant role in this journey. According to a Gallup poll, only one in three employees trust their manager.[96] Command-and-control leadership is one driving force that has strained trust. This style took hold in the US as World War II military leaders became business and institutional leaders upon their return home and used the lessons they learned in the military to lead.[97] Telling someone what to do does not build trust or inspire engagement, yet it still

---

95 Michael Bucy, Adrian Finlayson, Greg Kelly, and Chris Moye, "The 'how' of transformation," *McKinsey*, May 9, 2016.

96 Jim Harter, "Why Some Leaders Have Their Employees' Trust, and Some Don't," *Gallup*, June 13, 2019.

97 Robert Glazer, "'Command and Control' Leadership is Dead. Here's What's Taking Its Place," *Inc.*, August 12, 2019.

happens. People want to be involved in the processes and decisions and want to be a part of progress.

Another issue is our parents embedded in us from a young age that in our education and careers, decisions are made from the top down. We know and trust this method. Not because it's right, but because we've been anchored to this idea our entire lives. An adult elephant tied to a small stake could easily break free but does not.[98] It's been tethered by that same rope since it was an infant. The elephant has never escaped the rope before, so it assumes it never could as long as the rope is snug on its ankle.

"I've failed before, why would it work now?" In our careers we are tethered to following orders.

This shackle of being a follower can be efficient in the short term, but it is rarely effective further out for building a business. It quiets innovation and sets policy for the lowest common denominator. This is not a good standard to set. Typically, these policies are activity based and are set to avoid termination. This creates worker drones instead of policies inspiring excellence, promoting calculated risk taking, and encouraging growth.

The correct question isn't why are we fearful, but why aren't we more afraid? What's going on here?

---

98   Ryan Holmes, "The Elephant and the Rope: One Mental Trick to Unlock Your Growth," *Inc.*, January 30, 2017.

As careers develop, likely so does the value of one's input. But many managers stifle that. Why?

- Institutionalization: This is how we've always done it!
- Invulnerability: I must have a monopoly on good ideas!
- Insecurity: If we go with your idea, what's my role here?

Often, leaders don't intentionally act this way, it is merely a result of the culture the leader lives in. This further demonstrates that inspiring someone to evolve without trust is no easy task. Philip Holt, studio head at Undead Labs, a subsidiary of Xbox Game Studios, has faced institutionalization his entire career. When he hears this argument, Holt shared, "This is the first place I need to explore change." However, "before you implement change you have to spend time understanding your team members and building trust."

There may be a good reason to repeat a process or idea and there may not. It needs to be examined and you need buy-in if you feel change is necessary. Repetition can create comfort but does not ensure survival in any industry. This approach of reexamining can induce fear but is a necessary exercise to increase a company's chances of success. There are key methods to employ in leading change, grounded in empathy and vulnerability which we will explore later.

"The price of doing things the same old way is far higher than the price of change"

—PRESIDENT BILL CLINTON

Early in my career I worked on the sales desk of a mutual fund company in the 2 World Trade Center building, focused on actively managed funds. Times were good, but we had no index funds in the late 90s and were experiencing our first taste of industry disruption. John Bogle, the father of indexing, had launched his crusade for low-cost index funds in 1975.[99] The ramp up was slow in the early years, but that began to change as index performance improved.[100] Index funds ballooned from $4 billion in 1990 to $270 billion by the end of the decade, and this was just the beginning.[101]

Call after call rang in from clients and prospects asking, "Do you have index funds?" We retorted, "No, we believe in active management." I'll never forget that recurrent clicking sound from the other end of the phone line, followed by the lonely moan of a dial tone. The tidal wave of change was still far off-shore, but it was gaining momentum. With wide margins, it's easy to maintain old strategies and assume things will return to the old normal. In August of 2019, index fund assets surpassed those of actively managed funds for the first time.[102]

At the end of 2019, the consultancy Deloitte shared, "Seeking growth in an increasingly dynamic and complex industry

---

99 Jeanne Sahadi, "Vanguard's John Bogle dies at 89. Father of the index fund, he brought investing to the masses," *CNN*, January 17, 2019.

100 Ibid.

101 Paul Lim, "Investors Put Index Funds, if Not Their Theory, Into Practice," *LA Times*, September 26, 1999.

102 Alicia Adamczyk, "Index funds are more popular than ever—here's why they're a smart investment," *CNBC*, September 19, 2019.

landscape, investment management firms may need to leave comfort zones behind to explore new or different avenues next year."[103] The active money management industry continues to fight for relevance today as assets fly at warp speed from active to passive funds creating net outflows of money for many. Several asset managers have pivoted to Exchange Traded Funds (ETFs) and index funds, yet Vanguard index funds and ETFs now hold over three trillion dollars.[104] There are winners in the actively managed space, but margins are shrinking as low-cost options pressure fees and companies remain tethered to antiquated high-cost structures.

The value proposition of these firms needs to evolve rapidly, and many are making an effort. Change is often most difficult when profits are high. Since the Great Recession, a nearly twelve-year bull market has increased assets under management for most firms, masking the need to evolve. Some change has occurred in the industry since 2008, yet 242 of the largest 500 asset managers dropped out of the ranking by 2018.[105] With the meteoric rise in the markets, these asset managers have either chosen not to adapt to change or they have not found a suitable path forward and had to close their doors or begin to search for an exit as they bled assets.

---

103 Doug Dannemiller and Sean Collins, "2020 investment management outlook," *Deloitte Insights,* December 3, 2019.

104 "Not all index funds are created equal," Vanguard Corporation, accessed August 15, 2020.

105 Bob Collie, Marisa Hall, Tim Hodgson, Roger Urwin and Liang Yin, "The world's largest fund managers - 2019," *Thinking Ahead Institute,* 2019.

Change often seems appealing and novel until it forces you from your comfort zone and the novelty vanishes. There is no one single way to consider and drive adoption for change but it's often necessary. Andy Grove, former CEO of Intel, shared his view on change: "Only the paranoid survive."

Anyone operating in the business world should live with a little paranoia knowing that competitors are lurking in the distance. However, internal pressure from poor leadership is often the default mode, increasing fear in employees and keeping them from finding their next breakthrough. Building a team that is willing and able to work together around a common purpose can create a far more stable environment and more effectively drive long-term results.

Fear is a natural reaction to change or the idea of change. You will be facing something new in the form of your power structure, your job, the need for new knowledge, or replacing an old product or service. Common behaviors will have to evolve and that means more effort on your behalf and increasing your chance of failing along the way. The reality is people are often willing to embrace change, but if they don't live in a world anchored in trust, it's difficult to lead them through the process. As a leader, you need to shift your mindset. Consider the views of one great American leader:

"You manage things; you lead people."
—NAVY REAR ADMIRAL GRACE MURRAY HOPPER.

Many leaders are ill-equipped or undertrained to navigate this disruption and have not taken the time to alleviate that problem by building trust with employees. If people don't trust their leaders, their fear level will increase rapidly when change arrives. Leaders need to consider the power of serial optimization, engaging their team in the journey and taking their teams through a series of explained small steps, rather than talking about radical change from day one. Change is a necessary force and is headed your way; resistance is futile.[106] It's how you shepherd it and engage your team and learn along the way that makes the difference.

Optimization is a powerful force with many benefits, and we will explore these in the next chapter.

---

106 Robert Atkinson, "Resistance is Futile," interview by Ramtin Arablouei and Rund Abdelfatah, *Throughline*, NPR, April 25, 2019, audio, 37:01.

CHAPTER 3

THE POWER OF
THE OPTIMIZER

EPIC FAILURE

Join me on a journey back before the dot-com bubble. Yes, life before the year 2000, or Y2K as it was called, was a simpler time when your mobile phone couldn't provide access to every bit of information in the world, and its greatest feature was just making phone calls. I was enjoying life in New York City, finally earning enough money to cover the cost of living in my 250-square-foot studio apartment on the Upper East Side. It was early 1999, and I was in the midst of taking my Wall Street mentor's advice to expand my skill set outside of my company while fundraising for the New York Underground Film Festival (NYUFF).

My target audience was companies marketing their brand to the Gen X crowd—my crowd. One day, a friend told me about a company delivering goods right to your door from a website order and I said, "There's no way." My friend replied, "It's real; it's called Kozmo.com and they promise one-hour

delivery from website orders for no fee." They were growing like mad and had raised $280 million in venture capital
funding.[107] A cash sponsorship from Kozmo seemed like a
perfect fit to complement the money and twenty-two cases
of Jameson Irish Whiskey I had already secured. I tracked
down their marketing personnel to discuss sponsoring the
NYUFF and we met.

After a few chats about sponsorship, my contact told me they
didn't see the festival as a good fit. "But," he added, "we are
looking for a head of sales. What do you think about joining
Kozmo?"

This was intriguing, as it was late in 1999 and dot-com companies were all the rage. California had Silicon Valley and
NYC had "Silicon Alley."[108] Silicon Alley firms were disrupting the landscape of work and life in NYC, long dominated by
the patterns of financial services. My employer begrudgingly
allowed a casual work environment after years of suit and tie.
I was truly torn about leaving the comfort of Wall Street to
join a hip new venture, especially since I was finally making
decent money for a twenty-six-year-old.

A week later, I agreed to meet with my Kozmo contact to
explore employment terms. We met around 9:30 p.m., got a
soft drink at a bodega near their NYC office, and talked while

---

107 Kathy Bryan, "Kozmo: Bad Idea or Ahead of Its Time?" *Digital Marketing
News*, August 14, 2018.

108 Fergal Gallagher, "The Mysterious Origins of The Term Silicon Alley
Revealed," *Built In NYC*, November 4, 2015.

we walked. He spent thirty minutes endlessly discussing how well things were going at Kozmo. *I'd be crazy not to jump on board*, I thought.

On a dimly lit corner in the East Village, I finally stopped, turned to him, and asked:

"What is the deal you're thinking about?"

He paused, looked me right in the eye and said, "Thirty thousand dollars, plus discretionary stock options."

"That will barely cover my rent after taxes," I replied.

"You'd be a great fit and we need help growing!"

"Thanks, but I can't do it."

I began my deflated walk toward the number four subway station to head home. It would have been such a big risk, as I had no safety net, but I still couldn't help keeping tabs on Kozmo's progress.

Within the next year, they had over three thousand employees and entered several major cities. I was devastated for months that I passed this opportunity by. However, while Kozmo added over four hundred thousand customers, they still had not found a way to make money while burning through the entire $280 million from investors. In April of 2001, they permanently shut their doors after four years.

As the successful wine merchant Tim Varan once told me, "You can only sell a dollar for ninety-five cents for so long before it's a problem." I dodged a bullet and learned early in my career that enthusiasm doesn't always equal success, and I learned there was a limit to my risk tolerance.

NAIL IT BEFORE YOU SCALE IT

Peter Mellen, a serial entrepreneur and founder of Netcito, began attending the Georgetown University MBA program in the fall of 1996 with a focus on entrepreneurship. He was looking to build on the success he found in an earlier company he launched outsourcing IT work, but a mentor suggested he needed more knowledge.

On the first day in a marketing class, he found himself captivated by a single question the professor used to start a discussion.

"Where do you go to get ideas for new products and to innovate?"

Peter's mind was blank. He sat quietly, gripping his pen anxiously awaiting the answer.

"The customer!" the professor proclaimed.

Peter looked down at his notebook and wrote "customer." He stared at his page, wondering, "How could a customer help with new business building ideas?" He continued to ponder that question and think about his next company.

During his MBA program, he and a classmate wrote a business plan in an entrepreneurship class. With the plan, they raised fifty thousand dollars from investors to start a new company, Headlight, Inc. Just after graduation in 1998, they moved to San Francisco to build a team and grow.

This happened two years after Alan Greenspan, Chair of the Federal Reserve, coined the phrase "irrational exuberance" in reference to the overvaluation he saw in asset prices.[109] Headlight had strong appeal to investors as it was built to offer a "modern" form of training: online. The target audience was small- and medium-sized companies in need of a wide variety of hard and soft skills, and competition was thin.

Peter was able to raise an additional fifteen million dollars from one of the most prestigious venture capital firms in the industry, Draper Fisher Jurvetson, and it turbo-charged his company. He still had not spoken to a single customer or prospect. Why did they invest in a company run by a freshly minted MBA? In 1998, a *Harvard Business Review* article called "How Venture Capital Works" shared this perspective: "The myth is that venture capitalists invest in good people and good ideas. The reality is they invest in good industries."[110]

---

109   Kimberly Amadeo, "Irrational Exuberance, Its Quotes, Dangers, and Examples," *The Balance*, May 30, 2019.

110   Bob Zider, "How Venture Capital Works," *HBR*, November-December 1998.

In 1998, internet traffic was growing at a blistering 100 percent rate each year.[111] Investors wanted in and were pouring into a broad array of internet-based companies, such as the epic failure Pets.com that squandered over one hundred million dollars, mostly on ads that did little brand or business building.[112]

Peter's new company was right in the crosshairs at this time, with an incredibly opportunistic "internet-based" idea and the added benefit of a bright founder with a track record. There was no sock-puppet mascot like Pets.com, but a vision for a new way to efficiently provide employee training.

Peter learned the hard way that his marketing professor was correct. You must know your customer and the problems they need solved before you fully commit yourself to a solution. You need a viable product or service that can generate profits as you grow. Or, "Nail it before you scale it."

By March of 2001, Peter found himself liquidating Headlight, securing a total loss for his investors and leaving dozens without a job in the midst of a major economic recession. The baggage of this outcome took Peter years to unpack. After much reflection, he took the customer-focused lessons to heart used them to coach hundreds of entrepreneurs to successfully launch their own companies.

---

111 K.G. Coffman and Andrew Odlyzko, "The Size and Growth Rate of the Internet," *First Monday*, 1998.

112 "The 50 Worst Internet Startup Fails of All Time," *Complex*, October 18, 2020.

The sting comes right back every time he thinks about how little they focused on understanding their customers and how having a large pool of money sloshing around can be detrimental to investors and inexperienced business leaders. There is a better way.

LEAN STARTUP MOVEMENT

How Did We Get Here?

In the first quarter of 2000, venture capital firms set the lifetime record for the number of deals funded (2,277) valued over thirty-four billion dollars.[113] By the end of 2002, these record numbers plummeted over 85 percent to 315 deals and three billion dollars.[114] These results weren't unique to the private investment markets during the bubble burst. By the close of 1999, the technology-heavy NASDAQ stock index was up a record 84 percent and questions of stock prices going too far too fast began to circulate.[115] By October of 2002, the NASDAQ dropped 80 percent from its peak.[116]

These record losses understandably left many investors cautious of the next big thing, and it took over eighteen years to revisit these dizzying heights in the private markets. Only

---

113 Tom Ciccolela et al., "PwC MoneyTree Report," *PwC MoneyTree*, Q1 2020.

114 Ibid.

115 Brian McCullough, "A Revealing Look at the Dot-Com Bubble of 2000 — And How It Shapes Our Lives Today," *Ideas.TED*, December 4, 2018.

116 Ibid.

the fourth quarter of 2018 saw a higher level of investment than the peak of 2000.

After the dot-com bubble burst, investors unsurprisingly became more cautious and were far more reluctant to commit capital to unproven ideas. The number of deals funded has grown since the 2002 bottom, but the growth rate of the number of deals funded has far outpaced the value of deals funded.[117] Investors continued to explore new deals, they just weren't willing to pay as high a price for said risk. After watching friends abandon Wall Street to join companies that offered ping pong, an in office masseuse, and a robot to bring you a drink, I can't say I blame them.

Let's Get Lean

Startups don't fail only during economic recessions, they fail roughly 75 percent of the time.[118] Serial entrepreneur, Eric Ries, personally understands this pain of failure; he had to shutter the first company he and a college friend launched. In a later attempt in 2004 to develop a 3D instant messaging avatar company called IMVU, Ries was determined to increase his odds. Each of the founders had experience failing elsewhere and were determined not to fail again.

They asked bigger questions about their business idea. What should we build and for whom? What market could we enter

---

117   Ciccolela, "PwC MoneyTree Report."

118   Steve Blank, "Why the Lean Start-Up Changes Everything," *Harvard Business Review*, May 2013.

and dominate? After months of whiteboard sessions, building this new tool, and debating which features to keep, they launched their website—to no one.[119] They went back to fixing bugs and making improvements and still couldn't move the needle on sales.

After several more weeks and updates, they decided to pay potential customers for candid reviews of their idea face to face. They quickly discovered that their perceived magic trick for rapidly spreading their app through users was a point of resistance for their target audience. The idea was for the seventeen-year-old user to build their avatar and then invite a friend to do the same.

"Why?" they asked in one feedback session after another candidate refused to invite a friend.

The candidate replied, "I don't know if it's cool yet, so I can't risk inviting friends. If it sucks, they think I suck, right?"[120]

They retooled the product and gathered customer insights and buy-in along the way, finally finding the parabolic growth they desired. This feedback-driven approach minimized spending dollars and hours writing new code for what they believed customers wanted.

"Customers don't care how much time something takes to build. They only care that it serves their needs," Ries shared.

---

119 Eric Ries, "Creating the Lean Startup," *Inc.*, October 2011.
120 Ibid.

After this experience, they summarized the process they had uncovered: build, measure, learn—with a high sense of urgency. You can't just choose one from the list because each step must be taken and repeated regularly. For planning purposes, they found it is best to work in reverse. You start with what you want to learn, determine what should be measured to gain the knowledge, and then build, measure, and learn.

The Lean management approach is not new. Lean was coined in the late 1980s by researcher Jim Womack, PhD, to describe Toyota's car manufacturing process as a way to increase consumer value with fewer resources.[121] Ries had the unorthodox idea to bring it to the startup world.

Ries crafted this entire experience into the Methodology of Lean Start Up.[122] The keys are:

1. Eliminate uncertainty by continuously testing your vision with customers for a product or service.
2. Work smarter not harder by asking "Should this product be built?" not "Can this product be built?"
3. Develop a Minimum Viable Product (MVP). Figure out what problem you want to solve. Then build an MVP version of the idea to share with customers to learn from and further modify to meet their needs.
4. Validated Learning. Continue to ask questions and tweak the product until you understand what customers value.

---

121 Staff Writer, "What Is Lean." *Lean*, accessed May 15, 2020.

122 Eric Ries, "The Lean Startup Methodology," *The Lean Startup*, accessed May 16, 2020.

The concept is rooted in understanding the customer. New ideas are often focused on the creator's solution rather than the customer's problem. This leads to time wasted debating who's correct, rather than directly engaging the audience you want to serve to increase your chances of creating something they will actually purchase. Peter Mellen shares that another benefit to the iterative approach is it allows the focus to be shifted away from "Whose idea was this?" to "What have we learned about our customer to move our business forward?" This moves the conversation to problem resolution rather than placing blame.

YES IS THE ANSWER

Andy Grant has always had an entrepreneur's mindset along with his extraordinary technical skills. Marry these traits with a good guy who can just talk to people and you have the makings of someone truly unique. He started out in corporate America with a background in software and electrical engineering. He often found himself assigned to teams with the most sophisticated projects. Wherever he worked, the company always had him work on innovative projects set to launch in two to three years. In 2003, he found his then employer, ADC Telecommunications, shrinking their workforce by roughly 80 percent. He and his team of special project engineers survived dozens of rounds of layoffs before the news finally came in the spring of 2003 that their team was out.

The group gathered at a favorite beer hall on their last day to reminisce about their great run at ADC, and to consider what was next. Andy looked around the group of eight, held up his beer and said, "We've got a solid group here; why don't we build something together?"

The entire team plus his former boss set off to build a new product. They explored a number of options and opted to target the growing demand for high school and college kids to use instant messaging and music-sharing on their computers through a service called Napster.

The team launched a company in the summer of 2003 called yFire to build a new product that would get kids off their computers and onto a handheld gadget. The non-smart iPod portable media player had already launched, but the iPhone was still four years away.[123] They were onto something with yFire and they knew it. They began building a device and seeking funding to build a real prototype just one year removed from the bottom of the dot-com disaster. Every investor liked their idea but wanted someone else to do the seed funding. After a year, ADC severance packages were getting thin and the group broke up.

Andy rejoined corporate America and found himself rising through the ranks of an engineering consulting firm called WynEdge. His first project was as a subcontractor for 3M. They needed someone fluent in Visual Basic programming and Andy was the perfect fit. He loved the project and treated it like his own. Before long, 3M requested Andy to lead the project and his manager took notice. He was soon leading

---

123 Owen Andrew, "The History and Evolution of the Smartphone: 1992-2018," *Text Request*, August 28, 2018.

a team as a player coach, managing client relationships and also tasked with finding new business contracts.

This was a good taste of running a company and he quickly saw the value of keeping clients happy by soliciting feedback and engaging them in finding a solution. He wore many hats and relished the opportunity. The learning experience was transformative, the projects intellectually challenging and constantly changing. He saw how a wide range of companies worked, but, as a consultant, he was able to stay clear of much of the office politics and continue to learn from his clients' good and bad decisions. He wondered, "Is there a business opportunity here?"

After about six years, he felt the itch to start a new company again. He started attending startup events in Minneapolis and found just the energy he needed from his new network. After a year of spending evenings and weekends immersed in the startup scene, his big consulting contract came to an end. It was a perfect time to leave and start fresh. He rented a desk at a coworking space, CoCo, in the old Grain Exchange Building in the heart of the city.

He soon met John, a sales guy with a big idea. John had a problem though; he had no idea how to build his vision. Andy could build and John could sell. This was a fit worth exploring. They created VoiceHive in late 2012. This is a tool to facilitate stronger engagement with meetings and conferences. They knew they had something good after receiving rave reviews from presenting the concept at a pitch competition. They used several aspects of the Lean Startup methodology and still have not taken a dime from any investors.

Their early tool was unique in the market at the time. What was more unique was the chassis that Andy built, allowing great flexibility in what they could offer clients. It was an ever-growing Minimum Viable Product. Most conference technology options to this day are very black and white.

Their ability to adapt on the fly caught the attention of a few event planners and their business accelerated. What event planners liked is that VoiceHive could be largely customized to solve any client meeting need and make conference attendance more interactive—something few apps can do.

Andy and John developed a mantra:

> *"Yes is the answer. Now what is the question?"*

This customer centric approach has allowed them to grow steadily. Their success came not just because their product is unique, but because they take the time to understand the real problems their clients face and offer solutions. As they offer solutions, they engage the client in the process to ensure there is value in what they're building before they fully commit to the build.

Andy shared that, seven years later, "the company still runs lean with only seven employees and still no investors." Based on client demand, they diversified the revenue stream far from where they started. They have a highly recurring and growing client base because they take the time to understand the true needs of each client and work to collaboratively optimize a solution to every problem. One customer testimonial said, "I have been very pleased each time I have used VoiceHive, they are a delight to work with. The team can meet any challenge I set before them."[124]

* * *

Why iterate to optimize?

The lessons of the dot-com bubble burst still linger in the minds of many. Investing in companies that draw mountains of attention to their websites but can't find a path to profitability, die much quicker deaths today if they ever get off the ground. The losses were so large that a huge reset was placed on the risk assessment of starting a new business. These ideas aren't limited to starting a brand-new company, they can also be introducing a new product or process inside of an existing company. Established companies can also deliver epic failures, as we'll discuss later.

Eric Ries solidified for investors and entrepreneurs that you need to understand the problem that you're solving for your customer. It is only then that you can deliver quality and value. Without that direct knowledge from the customer, you are simply guessing and hoping that what you've created is loved by many people who are willing to give you their money. To do this, take the advice of Eric Reis and build your MVP, decide what to measure, learn from customers, know where they find value, and repeat every week.

---

124 "Here's what our clients have to say." VoiceHive, accessed May 13, 2020.

In part two, we will explore the principles of the Optimizer mindset and how they've proven successful despite ever-present obstacles.

PART 2

PRINCIPLES OF THE OPTIMIZER MINDSET

CHAPTER 4

VULNERABLE

"Vulnerability is the birthplace of innovation, creativity, and change."

—BRENÉ BROWN

On April 1, 1994, a hot stock investing tip appeared on *Prodigy*, an early internet site, that would change the wealth of investors for generations.[125] Chat rooms lit up with a flurry of activity. The company was Zeigletics, a sewage-disposal company in Africa. Many tried to buy the stock but couldn't; it was fictitious. This was an April Fools' Day prank. The story was soon covered by the *Wall Street Journal* and *Forbes* magazine.

America Online (AOL), an early internet provider, discovered this prank was pulled by two current subscribers. Brothers David and Tom Gardner were running an informal

---

125 Selena Maranjian, "15 Years of Fooling Around," *Fool.com*, Updated
     April 5, 2017.

investment forum on AOL, The Motley Fool. This stunt revealed they weren't afraid to look foolish in order to educate people while amusing them, like a court jester. Timing was good, as AOL was seeking content to increase their subscriber base of under one million.[126] They quickly sent their president to try to secure the brothers to a contract as hosts on an AOL investing forum.[127]

The Motley Fool co-founder David Gardner is a high-energy guy with a self-deprecating sense of humor and humility. He and his brother Tom both studied writing in college, so creating the early version of their newsletter the *Fool* came naturally. They covered sports and culture and soon added stock ideas for a forty-eight-dollar subscription fee in July of 1993, largely for friends and family.

Gardner shared that the Motley Fool's name is a nod to act 2, scene 7 of Shakespeare's *As You Like It*. A motley fool was the court jester that wore colorful attire, entertained the king, and most importantly, spoke the truth to all through humor. The brothers wanted to speak the truth about investing to everyone, while also having a bit of fun.

Righting a Wrong

The April Fools' joke was in response to the proliferation of "pump-and-dump" schemes being generated on this new electronic platform of the internet. Pump and dump is an

---

126 CNBC.com staff, "Timeline: AOL through the Years," CNBC, May 12, 2015.
127 Ibid.

illegal activity where you buy a low-priced stock in your own account, then promote the stock to many others to drive the price up and quickly sell your shares, likely leaving the others with a loss. The internet made this scam much easier to pull off. Rather than using a phone, you can contact many people very quickly with email or a social media post.

The brothers despised this scam and used their prank to expose it. They have carried on the April Fools' tradition ever since to help keep their office culture light in stark contrast to more traditional investment firms and to let their team know they are not afraid to be seen as a fool. As a leader, it sends a powerful message to your team when you have the courage to be vulnerable, especially to protect clients.

With their new AOL contract in hand and a rapidly growing community, Billionaire Ted Leonsis, former President of AOL, called them "the first generation of cyber-celebrities."[128] They were offered a revenue-sharing deal based on subscribers' time spent in their forum as payment. In 1994, AOL had a near monopoly for online use charging customers four dollars per hour. The revenue deal made the Motley Fool cash flow positive from day one.

The AOL money allowed Motley Fool to quickly hire. They started hiring friends, which helped set a less formal workplace culture. As they've grown, a key element of the company has always been a more casual environment—one

---

128 Benjamin Wofford, "The Motley Fool Is 25 This Year. Here's How They Changed the Way America Invests," *Washingtonian*, April 1, 2019.

that engages their audience and employees, embraces vulnerability, and gives them a voice in this new and unique community.

Gardner shared how transparency has always been part of their mindset, beginning with their early AOL chat room message to their audience: "Let's figure out the stock market together. We're not experts. We hope you'll answer our questions too." This was a strong and confident pivot away from traditional firms where information largely traveled in one direction, to the client. This fresh approach had broad appeal. In 1996 they were on the cover of *Fortune* magazine.

Even though they were feeling good about their financial start, David explained they still "didn't realize they were creating a company." But once they were featured on AOL, they had a platform to build an investor community and wanted to make it awesome. Like many innovations before them, they soon found negative sentiment about their new investment advice venture. Engaging the customer like a club member was new and disruptive. This negativity was fear-based.

Early on, their mission wasn't quite clear yet and they found themselves "starting from a David position against the Goliath of Wall Street, and online media, the Fool, was demeaned consistently by big journalism." At the same time, other investment forums were "hyping stocks in [their] niche" keeping fears of the pump-and-dump schemes alive. This challenged their credibility further and only fueled their fire to push their new business model forward.

Their unique approach continued to attract new customers and employees. Subscribers got free stock advice, as discount brokers financed the advice with ads to execute trades with their firm, and employees were having fun at work. David shared, "We needed ads, as most everything had to be free on the web in the late 1990s. That was our model."

They kept working to improve their offering and attract new clients. Soon they were offered a book deal which quickly became a best seller in 2001. Then the dot-com bubble burst and the party ended.

They quickly learned a hard lesson. "Your clients are those that pay you," David shared. Not one subscriber paid them and with ad sales dropping, difficult choices had to be made. They laid off 75 percent of their staff.

Ad sales recovered over the next few years and they began to explore a new subscription business model in 2007. Having been free for years, they knew this was a risk, but they again put themselves at risk of failure. Fortunately, thousands agreed to pay, and The Motley Fool was no longer tethered to ad revenue. The Great Recession of 2008 arrived the next year, but they were better positioned to weather the storm with recurring revenue.

"I think it was good timing. I don't want to give us too much credit."

–DAVID GARDNER

Stock markets dropped roughly 50 percent and employees were anxious about what was next. Tom and David knew transparency was needed to calm nerves and called a town hall meeting. They stood before all to announce that there would be no layoffs.

They showed extreme openness yet again and asked for everyone's help: "How are we going to cut costs to survive?" Their level of vulnerability gave them the courage to provide full transparency of the challenge ahead, empower everyone to join the cause, and free their minds to let creativity flow.

Every employee pitched in and sought ways to cut costs until business improved. This is what great leadership does: inspire team members to unite and solve problems together. They didn't look to cut costs in any one group. The plan was to share the pain together. A sign of this solidarity was choosing to pause the 401k matching benefit for everyone. As business recovered, they paid everyone the forgone match. Incredible!

Finding Their Way
From that day forward, they began to reflect on their larger mission. After a few iterations, they landed on: "Make the world richer, smarter, happier." There is no end. You can always do more. They've built optimization and innovation into their calling. Every single day employees ask, "What can I do to deliver our mission to clients?" Progress is in their culture; they can't undo it at this point.

The vulnerability of asking for help in 2008 earned the leadership great respect and trust from the team, and, now having a strong purpose, they were able to focus on a truly collaborative growth strategy. To maintain trust and unrelenting engagement, they consistently solicit feedback from all employees and work diligently to address any major concerns by the next survey period.

Many organizations write mission statements that sound good. Few have leaders willing to give their employees a true voice and the power to drive change, like The Motley Fool does. Today, they have nearly five hundred employees, multiple lines of business, a foundation, and over one million subscribers.

Teresa Amabile from Harvard Business School has researched employee engagement, and her work confirms The Motley Fool is on to something. She found that, more than anything else, employees want to make progress and contribute to meaningful work.[129] They want to matter at the place they spend over half of their waking hours. Managers' everyday actions make a difference in catalyzing or inhibiting this progress in engagement, and The Motley Fool has built this philosophy into the mission and culture.

Vulnerability doesn't happen automatically. A leader's vulnerability comes through self-awareness. Let's explore the key elements.

---

129 *TED Talks*, "Teresa Amabile: The Progress Principle," October 12, 2011, video, 18:36.

SELF-AWARENESS

The ability to recognize and understand your moods, emotions, and drives, as well as their effect on others are all components of Emotional Intelligence (EI). According to EI Author Dan Goleman, people with strong self-awareness are more even-keeled because they understand how their emotions impact them, others around them, and their careers.[130] They never get too high or too low emotionally and possess some hallmark traits.[131] What are they?

Self-Confidence

As a new manager hosting my first offsite meeting several years ago, I was given an unvarnished glimpse of self-confidence without self-awareness. We packed about fourteen people in a small hotel conference room around a U-shaped table. We had a full agenda, and I felt everyone was primed and ready to engage. I had a lot to learn, however.

No matter what topic came up, there was one person, we'll call him Brad, that dominated every discussion. Side conversations kindled around the room as the others disengaged.

Just before lunch we had an industry expert join us to share his insights. Everyone was particularly interested in the session but every time he paused, Brad peppered him with questions.

---

130 Daniel Goleman, *HBR'S 10 MUST READS: On Emotional Intelligence* (Boston: Harvard Business Review Press, 2015), Pages 4-21.

131 Ibid.

At the break, a long-time coworker of Brad's pulled me aside and showed me a t-chart with check marks largely on one side. "What is this?" I asked. "These are the times Brad spoke today versus everyone else," he shared. It was embarrassing.

As Brad was exiting the break area, I approached him.

"How do you think the meeting is going so far?"

"This is great!" he exclaimed.

"Brad, how would you gauge the level of engagement from your peers in our sessions?"

A blank stare came over his face. "I'm not sure," he said.

"Brad, I appreciate your level of enthusiasm for our meetings, but your peers haven't had much chance to participate."

"What do you mean?" he said.

"Brad, only you asked questions of our last guest."

"But my questions were relevant for everyone."

I made a simple request, "Brad, if you ask a question, count to ten in your head. If no one else speaks up, feel free to ask another." He begrudgingly acknowledged my request and the sessions improved markedly.

Self-confidence is the ability to know when to share your strengths and when to listen and learn. This genuine confidence comes with being honest with yourself.

Realistic Self-Assessment
A realistic self-assessment drives your ability to be self-confident. This insight gives you awareness of where you can and should contribute and helps others better appreciate your thoughts. This is challenging, as it forces us to admit a weakness in ourselves, but the effort can produce significant returns.

When this assessment is weak and one imposes their views on everything, it not only makes them less desirable to work with, but also makes the entire team feel they are not progressing or, worse, wasting their time. When this assessment is strong, it leads to curiosity about further self-improvement and more productive team interactions.

Thirst for Constructive Criticism
How can you know you've found a self-aware person? They are vulnerable enough to consistently ask for feedback. They ask questions like, "How do I get better and improve my results?" Or, "How can I bring more value to our relationship?" One team member I inherited in a reorganization feared constructive criticism. As opportunities presented themselves to offer feedback, it was always seen as a threat, and they grew more defensive.

The fear factor I saw was a solid reminder that I needed to deepen trust with that person, be more aware of our relationship, and better customize feedback. It's difficult to grow without being vulnerable enough to accept constructive feedback from your manager, peers, or clients, and feedback is rarely offered on an unsolicited basis. You need to seek this out yourself. We'll explore a road map for feedback later in the book.

Self-Deprecating Sense of Humor

Strong self-awareness allows you to not take yourself too seriously, and this sets a welcoming tone for your team to be engaged in every conversation. No one is perfect. Not being able to laugh about yourself can lead to disastrous results and a team afraid to speak up. And being able to laugh with others about yourself can bring people together and help build a high-functioning team. David Gardner of The Motley Fool is a great example of this. Without functional collaboration, it's difficult to deliver results. This form of humor, unfortunately, is often seen as weakness. The opposite is true. Being so comfortable and confident you can laugh at yourself builds trust and openness within a team.

Your team members don't want to follow you because you are their boss. They want to follow you and deliver results because they feel they have a voice in the journey and are comfortable sharing their views. Warren Buffett defines a leader as "someone who can get things done through other people." Your team will accomplish little innovation if you take yourself too seriously. Humor helps create a feeling of comfort at work and breaks down barriers to change.

Seeking feedback is not easy, but it can be embedded in your culture by exhibiting this behavior as a leader. You must show the way. Ask team members and peers to help determine how impactful you truly are.

If you can live with vulnerability and self-awareness, the next stage is even more impactful: empowering others.

EMPOWER OTHERS

Let's look at the power of vulnerability unfold in real life. Pulling each of these traits together, you find a common denominator for great leaders. They are vulnerable, self-aware and seek opportunities to empower others. It's not easy taking the back seat as the CEO, especially in a company that CEO founded.

Patti Brennan is a very caring, energetic person who never stops going and loves to solve puzzles. This dynamo, who stands just over five feet tall, was appointed captain of the women's college Lacrosse team at an NCAA Division I program and continually trains each morning before going to work. During the final year completing her nursing degree at Georgetown University (GU), instead of taking easy courses, Patti took a demanding financial planning course that offered very practical lessons on the subject. This class opened her eyes to a new world, but she followed her degree to nursing.

One night in the spring of 1984, she was doing rounds with a young resident and listened intently as he groaned about his pending income tax bill. Patti loved the challenge of doing her own taxes and shared a couple of actionable tax saving ideas. A perplexed look came over his face and he quipped, "What are you talking about?" Without hesitation, she replied, "Just give me your stuff and I'll do your taxes."

A few days later, Patti returned his tax forms with a two thousand dollar refund instead of a bill for one thousand dollars. Suddenly, Patti had a line of Residents at her nursing station with their tax forms in hand. As she walked the halls that night, she wondered if helping others with financial planning had potential.

A few months later, a sixteen-year-old boy was brought into her care. He was in a coma after a car accident. Several painful weeks went by with no sign of improvement. The family made the heart wrenching decision to let him go. They declined to come visit as they took him off life-support. With great sadness they said, "We want to remember Billy as he was alive."

They then asked a difficult favor of her: "Would you be with him at the end?" Patti obliged. She held his hand after he came off life support and realized the family made the right decision for themselves and that "there's no judgement in caring for another's needs."

By the next tax season, Patti was married and ready to explore her financial planning gift. In an industry with less than 20 percent women, and having no formal training, she applied for an account executive position with a new financial planning firm.[132] Her enthusiasm to help others, work ethic, and potential network were compelling enough to give her a shot. They offered her a job with a comparable compensation deal, with one small twist; it was a draw, not a salary. A draw is a monthly paycheck. If the monthly commissions you generate don't surpass the draw you were paid, you owe the firm the difference. Patti learned a new form of pressure, one she knew didn't align her interests with those of her clients.

Patti's business grew quickly through referrals as she took the time to truly understand her clients' needs, solve valuable problems, create a plan and make the complex simple. She continued to grow as a top performer in the office but after four years at this firm, Patti found a philosophical difference between herself and the senior partners of her company. They wanted to focus on high-net-worth clients and the former nurse couldn't wrap her head around not helping someone in need. They parted ways amicably and Patti moved her office into her home.

Now on her own, growth continued, and she soon had a team of fifteen working out of her basement with her four young children upstairs. She was no longer simply a financial planner; she was the CEO of a rapidly growing business and household. How did she keep it all going? With a simple philosophy: "As long as you focus on the next right thing,

---

132 Steve Garmhausen, "Women Make Great Financial Advisors. So Why Aren't There More?" *Barrons*, updated June 8, 2019.

taking care of your clients, be a little creative in thinking 'outside the nine dots,' you can make it work."

The nine dots are an old skill test she learned from a mentor. You draw a square grid of nine dots and try to connect all nine with only four continuous lines. Patti has spent her entire career outside of those nine dots leveraging her creativity with incremental adjustments, relentlessly seeking opportunities to improve how she and her team deliver world-class service to clients.

Do you think outside of the box? Try to connect all the dots with only four continuous lines:[133]

133   Sam Loyd, *Sam Loyd's Cyclopedia of 5000 Puzzles Tricks and Conundrums: With Answers.* (New York: The Lamb Publishing Company, 1914), 380

Over the years, Patti's business has flourished as she never stopped learning or maintaining extraordinary awareness of her limitations and building a team to complement her skills.[134] There's power in humility and lifelong learning. If a client brings her a problem she can't solve, she boldly tells them she doesn't know the answer but quickly finds it and often discovers a new service or solution to draw other clients to her practice. "It's never a push, always a pull," as she says.

People want to work with Patti and her team because they "optimize your entire financial picture, not just your investment portfolio. Your investments are a means to and end: effective planning for a life well-lived incorporates so much more than just portfolio management."

A key element of her optimization process is the rare practice of empowering all twenty-five team members in the annual business-planning and goal-setting meeting. Every team member has a voice in answering the question, "Is our current client engagement model highly impactful?" If an improvement is found, they build a new plan and implement it.

For 2020, they evolved their client service team from a pooled service model to assigned relationships. This plan has quickly paid dividends and earned a few team members additional raises. With deeper client knowledge, they could offer much more meaningful advice.

---

134 Tomas Chamorro-Premuzic, "7 Leadership Lessons Men Can Learn from Women," *HBR*, April 1, 2020.

Patti was inducted into the Barron's Advisor Hall of Fame in late 2019.[135] There are roughly 120,000 full-time financial advisors in the USA, and merely 145 of those have qualified for this list—far less than 1 percent. This recognition is a tribute to Patti's hard work, sensitivity to customers and staff, and continual optimization of her business.

* * *

Vulnerability is about putting yourself out there and risking receiving feedback about yourself you have yet to discover. As a leader, you need to embrace vulnerability; let your team know you're not perfect and engage them in this feedback loop. This builds trust and creates an environment that is "compelling and not mandatory," as Kara Chambers, VP of Human Insights at The Motley Fool, puts it. There will always be times when you simply have to get a project completed or solve a problem. Revealing yourself to your team will make that effort far more engaging for all.

We will reveal a roadmap to developing this process in part three of this book. Join me in continuing to understand the optimizer mindset and problem solving.

---

135 Daniel Downey, "Barron's Financial Advisor Hall of Fame," *Barron's*, October 25, 2019.

PROBLEM SOLVER

ITERATE TO INNOVATE

"This isn't a meet and greet, it's an interview!" Philip realized as he sat in front of his potential new boss, Warren.

"Where do you see your value in the game industry?" Warren, a senior leader at Electronic Arts (EA) asked.

EA Vancouver is a premier game studio. In 1996, EA purchased his parents' video game company they had started in Philip's childhood home. After four years working for his parents, Philip explains he was now "reporting to someone who had no particular loyalty to his success." He quickly decided, "I better show this guy my value proposition." Warren liked Philip's energy and fresh ideas and decided to give him a chance. He assigned him to a project outside of his primary job, one with an existing sports game.

"We need to update our baseball game, *Triple Play*, and fix some bugs. Think you can do it?" Warren asked.

"Absolutely," Philip replied.

Knowing he needed help, he put together a team of three with diverse backgrounds to tackle this challenge.

A major skill Philip had was problem solving and course-correcting mid project, which is no easy task. Philip found a passion for solving dynamic puzzles after many experiences working in a restaurant kitchen. A chef-owner he worked for taught him, "Something will likely go sideways while preparing dozens of meals. You have to adapt and find a solution fast, or business will suffer." Philip discovered early on that learning is all around us.

Each team member on the special *Triple Play* project recognized the extraordinary opportunity and worked tirelessly to deliver quality. Together, they approached the project with great curiosity, not knowing what they'd find. They fixed bugs, added new features to the game, and shipped over four hundred thousand copies—far beyond expectations.

Shortly after, Warren phoned Philip. "Your work on *Triple Play* was remarkable."

"Thanks, it was fun," Philip replied.

On his commute home that night, Philip reflected on lessons learned. Warren was empathetic to a bright young man and gave him a chance. He also saw the value in empowering an ownership mindset. Philip and his team not only surprised Warren with their exceptional work, but they also surprised themselves with how they established roles and responsibilities, upgraded *Triple Play*, and dramatically lifted sales. The team validated what one of the world's greatest minds once said:

"It's not that I'm so smart, it's just that I stay with problems longer."[136]

Philip is not the most technical person. His unique abilities are problem-solving and his collaborative approach to leadership. He works with his team to fully understand a problem, establish a road map, goals, set guidelines, and empower the team to work and ask questions until they come up with a solid resolution.

Philip's career took off, as did the game industry. In 2005 he landed back at EA, this time in central Florida, the home of EA's *Madden NFL*. This was the number-one game of 2005 and 2006, selling over six million copies annually.[137] Philip's successful problem-solving soon earned him a top spot in the studio. He took the time to build strong relationships with his team members. However, in the next few years he found

---

136 Staff Writer, "The Hidden Habits of Great Problem Solvers," Korn Ferry Advance, accessed April 12, 2020.

137 Kevin Webb, "The Best-Selling Video Game of Every Year, from 1995 to 2019," *Business Insider*, December 25, 2019.

PROBLEM SOLVER · 97

himself increasingly at odds with the EA leadership and felt they treated employees poorly.

Weeks before Christmas in 2010, Philip received an unplanned request to meet with his boss. "We're restructuring the company and eliminating your position," Philip's boss said. A chill raced through his body and lingered for hours. With three young daughters and a mortgage, he was in a tricky position. He spent the holidays contemplating career options and chose to launch a new company. The timing felt right, as calls from former employees poured in asking to join his new venture.

Philip co-founded a video game and data analytics company with a former EA colleague. Philip and his co-founder spent months crossing the USA and pitching their idea to dozens of venture capital firms. They used each rejection to refine their story and eventually raised nine million dollars.

Now funded, they put yet another diverse, high-quality team together and launched. Their first game won a creative award, but they quickly discovered trophies don't always translate into sales. Burning through money, the "heat in the kitchen was high," and a pivot was necessary.

Philip asked everyone to take a pay cut, focus exclusively on the data business, eliminate game development, and continue to deliver excellence. His co-founder didn't agree and left. Knowing he needed to send a strong message to his team and investors, Philip took the largest pay cut.

The company experienced a glimmer of hope when they landed a small data analytics contract with a Fortune 500 company, but it was too little too late, and they closed after four years. Their investors lost patience with how quickly they went through money.

Philip and his family decided to move to Seattle to be closer to relatives. He leveraged his track record to secure a senior leadership position running one of Microsoft's most popular game studios. He succeeded the studio's founder and began optimizing with a team of nearly one hundred.

"Quality is key and the only way to get there is through a series of optimizations," Philip shared. He added, "Ideas are easy; the real work is in getting your team to nurture them into something awesome. Therefore, you must empower your team to challenge each other, allowing optimization to happen, solving problem after problem as they surface."

Philip has learned repeatedly that business will not progress in a straight line and you have to adapt, on the fly at times, and be audacious enough to try to operate outside of your comfort zone to get to the right solution.

Problem solving is a critical skill of the optimizer. Optimizers don't simply resolve issues; they continue to think creatively about the questions they ask, unearthing a deeper understanding of what's needed, and work tirelessly to deliver a quality result. Additionally, they establish a system and structure to avoid prematurely making judgements before they have a strong understanding of the true issues.[138]

CAN'T STOP

Nicole has a warm smile that lights a room and the passion to never stop improving. She was raised in a working-class family where her "father worked three jobs to support us. It was inspiring." She knew early on how hard he pushed himself to make the best life he could for his family. It wasn't an easy life.

She started babysitting at age twelve and earned W-2 wages at fourteen. A favorite babysitting customer said they paid her for every shirt she ironed after the kids went to sleep. The family always came home to their shirts neatly ironed on hangers and she'd ask, "What else can I help with?"

She loves the opportunity to push herself and do more, a focus her father gave her early on. He offered to buy her a car for her sixteenth birthday if she earned straight A grades. She did it, and found a used Chevrolet Chevette waiting for her in the driveway on her special day. She completed a similar challenge to get help with financing her college degree.

Her father knew education would create a future for his children that he never had. She explained, "He pushed me in ways that he wasn't able to push himself." He was often

---

138 Shale Paul, "The Top 10 Characteristics of Problem Solvers," Strategic Searches, September 24, 2017.

coming up with big ideas to solve problems, but never had the time to make them a reality. Nicole took her father's work ethic and creativity and her mother's eternal optimism and turned them into a career in financial services.

These skills may have been the perfect combination for a future superstar sales executive: a creative-minded hard worker who believed she could accomplish anything. Now she's married with four children, has a demanding professional life, and is a consistent top performer for her firm, raising over $750 million each year calling on financial advisors as her clients.

Part of her insatiable thirst to improve is a need for efficiency and a disdain for mediocrity, a perspective that her parents fostered with her education. To maintain an exceptional business and a healthy work-life balance, she needs to leverage her time effectively. This mindset does not keep her from experimenting, however: "Any idea I come up with has to address a client problem."

As an example, she created her own client segmentation service model years before her employer provided training on that very issue. She knew this would improve client retention and growth, so she did it on her own with the help of her team. To make it work, she also developed clear roles and responsibilities, establishing accountability for each team member and how they would contribute to their goals.

After developing mastery with her segmentation plan, she used that knowledge to coach her clients to do the same. She knew if she was going to coach someone on a specific topic, she needed a deep understanding and the best way to gain that knowledge was to do it herself.

The COVID-19 pandemic is a strong example of how she continues to evolve her thinking. You can't just solve the problem; you must push further. Always with an eye on the "client experience" she delivers, she shared, "If it's not customized for your top clients, it won't matter."

The pandemic has forced salespeople to stop seeing their clients face to face, which has been a significant setback for many. Some have been paralyzed, some have created a phone-based business plan, and others are waiting for a vaccine. This doesn't work for Nicole. She advised, "You have to be proactive about helping your clients. You have to make it easy for people to do business with you."

Within days of being in quarantine, she moved her in-person meetings to video conferencing and continued to dig into current client issues and work on resolutions. She worked as if things were normal, just on a video screen instead of in person, and found herself busier than ever.

"The early video calls were awkward," but she was determined to make it work. She asked for constructive feedback at the end of each call and had some simple early learnings from one client: "Your email ping is distracting." Being so used to the "ping" noise, she'd grown numb to it, but readily turned it off. Yet again, she found a problem in her business and worked tirelessly to find a solution by connecting the dots, oftentimes in an untraditional fashion.

Her video skills proved so successful that peers asked to learn from her and listen to her virtual meetings. She agreed to let them join but there was a price: "They had to offer me at least one idea on how to make the calls better."

A top client wanted to continue marketing their business with virtual meetings. They invited her to an upcoming weekly team strategy meeting. It is highly unusual for a successful financial advisory team to invite an outside sales executive to this type of meeting. They told her of plans for a virtual dining experience with a local chef for fifty clients.

She challenged them to make the event more intimate and do several dinners with smaller groups allowing clients to invite friends as potential prospects. They loved the idea and appreciated her thoughtfulness and willingness to guide them to a better solution. Attendees raved about the event and the financial advisors added several new clients they met through the dinners. The advisors have since asked Nicole to be a regular attendee at their strategy meetings.

She continues to confidently engage clients in a feedback loop to ensure she is delivering what they value. Months into the global pandemic quarantine, her business continues to thrive. She is already planning how she will leverage video conferencing to improve efficiency even after she can return to face-to-face meetings.

Her employer has recognized her by presenting her with numerous awards and inviting her to participate on an internal advisory board for the company. This board provides insights into the leadership team and is made up of top performers as well as those who see the business from an enterprise level and not only from their vantage point.

In addition to never slowing her effort to succeed, Nicole has developed the mindset to push herself persistently forward. The global pandemic has been just another challenge to optimize around. She finds formal and informal learning all around her, empowering her with further growth. This is one of the key elements of problem solving.

LIFELONG LEARNING

After earning a professional designation in my career, the Certified Investment Management Analyst or CIMA, my mind was opened to endless possibilities. It was no easy task, requiring about 250 hours studying over a year to get through it. Upon completion, I felt my brain more alive in an unfamiliar way and knew I had much more learning to do in the world.

The CIMA paid dividends from early on as I looked to apply my new knowledge each week. A sales meeting with a top prospect finally came through after several attempts. During the meeting, I learned they had analytical work done on an investment lineup for a proposal to bid on a 401k plan. The report was riddled with data, but they needed the short version.

With my new designation, I took the reports home for review and came back with detailed notes the next day. After years in the business and many of these reports sent their way, they confided that "no one had ever actually explained how to read them." They were very thankful and soon became perennial top clients for my business. This success convinced me that I should and could continue my learning journey, and I later earned an Executive Master of Business Administration (EMBA).

Problem solving does not come naturally to everyone, nor does serial optimization. Committing time in your life to continue your learning journey is a key element to empowering yourself and your team to live in the optimizer mindset. Let's look through the lens of the essential elements of lifelong learning according to Mckinsey and Company, a consultancy firm.[139]

Do What You Love and Discover Your Purpose

As Chris drove home from New York City to Connecticut on a Sunday night in the spring, he rolled the windows down to take in fresh air as the adrenaline from being on the UN stage still ran through his veins; his mind was racing.

During those two hours in the car he reflected on his participation in a Model UN challenge, where he found himself presenting in front of hundreds of attendees. *What did I just do? How did I become the leader of my team? Why did they listen to me?* His path to a life in politics was growing clearer.

---

139 Jacqueline Brassey et al., "Seven Essential Elements of a Lifelong-Learning Mind-Set," McKinsey, February 19, 2019.

After high school, Chris attended the University of Connecticut to study political science. In 1992, he graduated with honors and began to visualize his name on campaign signs. After graduation, he was hired to be a congressional aide at the US House of Representatives.

After two years as an aide, he could feel the need for further education to lend more credibility to his campaign story. He completed a master's program at Harvard University in organizational innovation and reform—a perfect skillset for a politician. After graduating in 1996, Chris truly found a new level of passion for learning.

Chris was accepted at Duke to earn his PhD and was assigned Professor Sim Sitkin (Professor of Leadership and Management) as his advisor. Professor Sitkin was already doing work on trust and control, which aligned well with Chris' PhD statement of interest. He shared, "Few professors at the time were doing research on the intersection of conflicting topics."

At his first meeting, Professor Sitkin handed Chris a paper from 1979: "A Conceptual Framework for the Design of Organizational Control Mechanisms" by William Ouchi.

Chris read the paper on the plane ride home and his mind was reeling. He stared blankly at the back of the chair in front of him and realized a political career wasn't his calling. His future was in academics and innovation. Not innovating gadgets, but "bringing new knowledge to the world that hadn't been seen before; this is innovation."

He continued his work off William Ouchi's paper on control and found the real value wasn't going deeper in one category, it was at the intersection of two areas of natural tension that needed exploration, trust, and control.

As he dug into this work he found, "If I'm overtly controlling you, you tend not to trust me. However, if one can effectively control an employee in a way that gains trust, that's really powerful." As he dug more deeply into the employee mindset, he also found that fairness needed to be part of his work and his dissertation was born.

After completing his PhD in 2002, he became a professor instead of running for office. He has now taught for nearly twenty years at prestigious schools, won awards for his research, and doesn't see politics in his future any time soon. He found his purpose as an educator by problem solving throughout his career journey and continuing to learn. He pushed himself to grow and now shares his passion for learning with students. He sees lifelong learning as having two major benefits:

> *"First, with education, you see that the world isn't as good as you thought it was. Second, there's a knowledge resource that you could apply to actually make your life significantly better."*

To realize these benefits, you need to push yourself beyond your normal capabilities. Let's look at an example.

Stretch Yourself

After several years of a successful marketing career, Micah opted to challenge herself and join a startup. She loved the rapid pace and soon felt the need to "accelerate her learning." In the summer of 2015, she decided that an MBA was the right fit. She started a weekend program in August. By the next spring, she was enjoying her newfound knowledge, but her employer lost funding and the company closed.

Thanks to a referral from her cousin, she was able to find a marketing position with Charles Schwab in the midst of her MBA program. After a few successful years with Schwab, she wanted something more. She sought mentorship from her manager, who not only encouraged her to push herself but opened doors for her across the firm to explore new career paths. She used this opportunity to secure several meetings with various department leaders. Through this journey, she found a promotion to a senior manager position with the corporate strategy team and is relishing the challenge.

Micah is an ideal mentee in many respects as she always has a well-researched target she's aiming for, which makes advice much easier to give. She takes the time to be highly specific in asking for help, making the mentor's work to guide her more impactful and efficient.

She continues to seek opportunities to put herself in positions where she has to stretch herself to keep up, while expanding her skillset and learning. She owns her development, and this is all done with a focus on growth and a goal of landing a chief marketing officer (CMO) role one day soon. She is well on her way.

* * *

Problem solving with a focus on learning is critical to the optimizer mindset. Where others see a setback, the optimizer sees a growth opportunity to expand their thinking. They will rarely be the "smartest person in the room," but they are willing to push harder, be ever curious, think outside the box, and find a better way to deliver customer value.

Next, we'll look at how a customer-centric focus is at the heart of how the optimizer finds a way to channel their energy and ideas to provide true value, keeping the customers coming back.

CHAPTER 6

CUSTOMER CENTRIC

———

HELP PEOPLE EAT BETTER AND LIVE BETTER

In 2006, the Chinese government announced an "indigenous innovation" campaign to establish China as a technology powerhouse by 2020.[140] One outcome of this effort was radical change in the food-delivery business developed by a new company, Meituan Dianping (MD). Chinese food delivery generated $86.2 billion in sales in 2019 and MD stood ready to deliver.[141] Between 2010 and the end of 2018, food delivery revenues had grown over 1,000 percent in China.[142]

MD has dominated the delivery business with an army of 600,000 delivery people and a target on improving the

———

140 Kenneth Miller, "Is China Winning the Innovation Race?" *Leapsmag*, June 19, 2018.

141 Emma Lee, "There Are No Food Delivery Winners," *Technode*, April 29, 2020.

142 Valeriia Mikhailova, "Food Delivery in China: A Rapidly Expanding Tech Battleground," *China Economy* (blog), *Daxueconsulting*, March 11, 2020.

customer experience, now capturing 60 percent of the Chinese market, making them the largest food delivery service on earth.[143]

Simply delivering food wasn't enough for MD. Thanks to their focus on growth in food and many other business lines, they were named the "most innovative company" of 2019 by *Fast Company* magazine for "pioneering transactional super apps."[144] A super app offers multiple apps in one, and MD now offers over 200 services.[145]

MD's founder, Wang Xing, has succeeded by placing extreme energy on understanding and solving a variety of customer demands. He's paid particular attention to those consumers in the rapidly growing Chinese middle class, estimated to reach 550 million by 2022.[146] Xing also emphasizes constantly optimizing every step of the value chain and expanding options, aspiring to be the "Amazon of Services."[147] Jeff Bezos, the CEO of Amazon, is a household name in America as is Amazon; but Mr. Xing and MD aren't yet.

---

143 Lee, "There Are No."

144 Eillie Anzilotti, et al., "The World's 50 Most Innovative Companies 2019," *Fast Company*, March/April 2019.

145 Josh Spero and Nian Liu, "Meituan Dianping Shows Route to Food Delivery Profits," *Financial Times*, December 15, 2019.

146 "How Well-Off Is China's Middle Class?" *China Power* (blog), updated August 26, 2020, accessed August 27, 2020.

147 Emma Lee and Nicole Jao, "Meituan Faces Challenge from Alipay on Its Home Turf," *Technode*, April 1, 2020.

Mr. Xing was born in 1979, the year before China began allowing private enterprise.[148] His father was an entrepreneur and built a successful cement company that helped improve China's infrastructure, and Xing found that inspiring.[149] Xing is a tall, thin man, always found with wire-frame glasses and a crew cut. After earning an undergraduate degree, Xing moved to the US for a PhD program in computer engineering to cultivate his passion for American innovation.[150] He dropped out after learning of Mark Zuckerberg's success with Facebook and began exploring business ideas with friends.[151]

Xing and his friends made several attempts at startups and eventually found a win with Xiaonei, the Facebook of China.[152] Xiaonei's success helped him finance Fanfou, a microblogging app similar to Twitter.[153] This credibility afforded him the option to launch Meituan in 2010.[154] The name means "Beautiful Together" and serves to constantly market the message of group discounts, and it is symbolic of Mr. Xing's rigorous optimizing.[155] Xing's track record garnered

148 Lulu Chen, David Ramli and Peter Elstrom, "The World's Greatest Delivery Empire," *Forbes*, March 28, 2019.

149 Jordan Schneider, "Meituan's CEO Wang Xing at 40, Without Doubts," *ChinaTalk*, June 21, 2019.

150 Yashica Vashishtha, "Wang Xing: Chinese Billionaire Businessman & the Founder of Meituan," *Your Tech Story*, April 6, 2019.

151 Ibid.

152 Gady Epstein, "The Cloner," *Forbes*, April 28, 2011.

153 Vashishtha, "Wang Xing."

154 Ibid.

155 Lulu Chen, David Ramli and Peter Elstrom, "The World's Greatest Delivery Empire," *Forbes*, March 28, 2019.

the attention of Sequoia Capital, a perennial top US venture capital firm.[156] They invested twelve million dollars in MD in 2010.[157]

His initial focal point was on simplifying food delivery and growth. In 2015, Meituan merged with Dianping, the Yelp of China, and MD was born.[158] The overall strategy was now in place, the "food plus platform," as Xing called it.[159] Alibaba had already dominated the sale of goods online in China, but service offerings had no clear winner.[160] Xing saw the opportunity. Thinking back to his father's contribution to China, Xing established a clear mission for MD:

"We help people eat better and live better."[161]

—WANG XING

156 "The Top 100 Venture Capitalists," *CB Insights*, March 31, 2019.

157 Vashishtha, "Wang Xing."

158 Yue Wang, "China's Meituan, Dianping Merge to Create A Mega Online-To-Offline Service Platform," *Forbes*, October 8, 2015.

159 Julie Zhu, "China's Meituan Dianping to Focus on Domestic Market after $4.4 Billion Hong Kong IPO," *Reuters*, September 6, 2018.

160 Daniel Laboe, "Alibaba Vs. Amazon: Who Will Take Over the World First," *Yahoo Finance*, April 8, 2019.

161 Kevin Zhou, "Meituan CEO Talked about Relationships with BAT," *Pandaily*, June 28, 2017.

He worked tirelessly to understand and better serve consumers under thirty-five years old, growing discretionary consumption spending by 14 percent each year.[162] (25).

From the day Meituan and Dianping merged, synergies accelerated with their app as they connected millions of new consumers to merchants through food delivery, restaurant reviews, and promotions. To draw both consumers and merchants away from incumbent service providers, they built an enormous delivery network to boost partnerships, adding over four hundred thousand local businesses to their platform.[163] Every delivery person carries a phone for real-time data to optimize routes.[164]

Everyone was winning. Merchants were growing their business, consumers were eating better, and MD was fulfilling their mission to improve life in China.

Mr. Xing maintained his insatiable appetite for efficiency across the enterprise, looking to streamline every department of MD. In the office, Xing sits in an open row amongst colleagues and computers, offers no free snacks or drinks and hosts interviews in the hallway, all to optimize his cost

---

162 Kim Iskyan, "China's Middle Class Is Exploding," *Business Insider*, August 27, 2016.

163 Vashishtha, "Wang Xing."

164 Yingzhi Yang, "China's Meituan Dianping Pushes Its Short Delivery Service to More Customers in Search for Profit," *South China Morning Post*, May 7, 2019.

structure.[165] His daily visibility serves as a constant reminder that everyone plays a part in evolving the business.

To help his merchant partners improve operations and drive robust growth, MD invested $1.65 billion in 2019.[166] MD made the investment to support merchants in their marketing efforts, digital upgrades, and supply chain services, as well as to provide awards and incentives for innovation.[167]

Leading change is never easy; financial incentives can help to drive adoption of the change and emphasize problem-solving for customer needs. MD leverages its platform to provide comprehensive services for merchants, including marketing, delivery, IT, supply chain, operations, and finance to meet merchants' business-upgrading needs, and to help improve the efficiency of its delivery ecosystem.[168] This was all done in the spirit of driving efficiency through every step of the supply chain and delivering a better customer experience and growth.

Living his mission, Xing always asks how he can improve services for his customers and their evolving needs. As their food delivery business exploded to number-one in China, he found travel demand growing and added hotel bookings to

---

165 Shai Oster and Yunan Zhang, "A Chinese Startup's Big Ambition: Amazon for Services," *The Information*, March 27, 2018.

166 "Meituan to Invest rmb11 Billion to Support Merchant Development," *PR Newswire*, January 23, 2019.

167 Ibid.

168 Ibid.

his app.[169] This business quickly rose to the top, and Xing continued his search for more service options to attract customers.[170]

In 2018, MD's 350-million-person customer base exceeded the entire US population. They offered a wide swath of services including catering, on-demand delivery, car-hailing, bike-sharing, hotel and travel booking, movie ticketing, and other entertainment and lifestyle services.[171] The opportunity set was ripe for further growth.

In the first half of 2018, MD executed 178 transactions per second—yes, *per second*—each day.[172]

Meituan Dianping had its initial public offering in 2018 and is now the third largest technology company in China, behind Alibaba and Tencent, with a valuation of $75 billion.[173] They rank fortieth on the Fortune 500 list, just behind retailer Target.[174]

---

169 Carol Yin, "Meituan Hotels Surpassed Ctrip to Lead the Online Hotel Booking Industry in q2 2018," *Pandaily*, September 3, 2018.

170 Ibid.

171 David Lidsky, "The 2 Most Innovative Companies in the World Today Are Changing How Hundreds of Millions of Asian Consumers Buy Food, Book Hotels, and (A Lot) More," *Fast Company*, February 19, 2019.

172 Ibid.

173 Tripti Lahiri and John Dextrixhe, "China's Favorite Food Delivery Service Is Now Worth More Than Its Biggest Internet Search Firm," *Quartz*, June 24, 2019.

174 "Fortune 500," *Fortune*, 2019.

With a constant emphasis on understanding his customer base, meeting their needs and driving efficiency to optimize his entire supply chain, Wang Xing, a newly minted Chinese billionaire, built an empire that will likely be a force for years to come. Mr. Xing's aspirations don't stop there, as his goal is to become the most important technology company in the daily lives of Chinese people.[175] Given his relentless focus on discovering customer needs and optimizing his operations to deliver, I believe he'll get there.

EMPATHY IS HIS SUPER POWER

Eric Horner was the youngest of four brothers that grew up in a modest home in Grand Rapids, Michigan, with his parents and grandmother under one roof. Eric has an infectious smile and laugh that draws everyone around him closer. This gift helped make him a fixture in school plays.

One day, he arrived home from school to his grandmother, very upset after not getting a part. She took his hand and slowly walked him to the couch. She let him catch his breath, looked into his eyes, and shared:

"Sorrow has its reward. It never leaves us where it found us."

Empathy plays a pivotal role in customer focus and Eric learned it early on. This gift has been instrumental to building his long-term success.

---

175   Yang Yang, "Meituan Makes Robust Stock Debut in Hong Kong," *China Daily*, September 21, 2018.

Many people spend their entire working lives wondering if they are in the right career; not interior designer Eric Horner. Both parents worked as sales representatives for luxury furniture lines in Grand Rapids, a.k.a. "Furniture City."[176] Being immersed in furniture during his upbringing, easily connecting with others, and having an innate ability to look at anything and be willing to ask, "Is there another way?" led to him to his calling.

When he was eight years old, his parents put an addition onto the house. The day after completion, Eric heard his mother struggling to fit their existing large dining table in the new room. He entered, took a quick look, and said, "Mommy, that won't work; the table has to be at an angle." His parents moved the table to the suggested angle to let him be part of the process. To their surprise, it worked perfectly, and big smiles flew around the room. That table sat at Eric's angle for the next ten years until they moved and every day it served as a reminder of his gift.

At twenty-eight years old, having a passion for entrepreneurship and a gift for design, he took the startup leap when an older friend asked him to form a company together. They quickly launched Brogan and Horner Interiors. Within a few years his partner wanted to retire, so Eric bought him out and has been in charge ever since. He has built a solid business of repeat and referred clients from all walks of life that always comment on his ability to "deliver what they want."

---

176 Tim Marklew, "Michigan's Grand Rapids Was Once Known as Furniture City," *Culture Trip*, May 7, 2018.

At age thirty-eight, Eric had three major projects canceled in one week. It was the only time he has been without work in his entire career. He pondered cutting staff, but decided to sleep on it, remembering his grandmother's sage wisdom: "Sorrow has its reward." The next day, he brought his smile to work, knowing his team needed a boost. As he unpacked his briefcase, his phone rang. It was a referral, Ted, from a long-time client and two-star general.

Ted was a high-profile client with a major problem. He was in Boston and needed immediate help on a large-scale historic home renovation as his contractor had been arrested for taking project deposits and not delivering work. Eric was on a plane the next day and realized that

"*in every business, there are landmark moments. Not only are you defined as a person, but the business is defined and it's never the same.*"

This trip was Eric's landmark moment.

Eric earned this referral; it was not luck. It was driven by his ability to listen and comprehend his clients' needs. This skill set has empowered him to build deep relationships, making him indispensable to his clients as he consistently exceeds expectations. He doesn't impose his style on your home. Through his consultative approach, he guides you to making your dream house come to life.

His multi-step process, which starts simply and powerfully with getting to know his clients and understanding their needs, enables him to see the goal through his clients' eyes and engage them right from the start. It's true collaboration. Eric gives everyone a voice in decisions, ensuring needs are met, just as his parents did for him with their kitchen table. When it's time to place an order with Eric, it doesn't feel like a sale since you're getting exactly what you want.

Thanks to his efforts, he is nearing thirty-five years in business, continues to grow through referrals, and has clients all over the US.

NEVER SACRIFICE SERVICE FOR VOLUME

Sometimes innovation isn't about new gadgets; it's about improving something tried and true.

Tim Varan has built the largest independent wine store chain in Florida over twenty-five years with wit, grit, and extraordinary customer service.

Tim grew up in western Pennsylvania. In high school, he witnessed 25 percent unemployment and "was really determined to never see that again." After graduation in 1985, he moved to Orlando to attend college. He worked full time through school, as that is what Varans did; they worked. Tim first waited tables at an Italian place and fell in love with food and wine.

After several months, he joined a casual gourmet-dining restaurant chain, Pebbles, where he met his first mentor,

David Webley, the general manager. David's belief was providing an exceptional customer experience to every guest. He ran extensive training and required that his staff bring superior service, solid product knowledge, and deliver a seamless presentation. Tim saw how this philosophy created a solid base of customers and drew others in. Upon graduation in 1989, he was offered a job in accounting with another wine merchant. He took the job but soon left after he found an opportunity to return to his passion for wine.

His new manager had a brilliant palette for wine and could spin captivating stories, but as Tim shared, "never once negotiated on price with distributors." Tim's wine knowledge grew, and he learned the power of consistent marketing as he built and grew a customer base by sending monthly wine newsletters to prospective clients, before email even existed. Within a few months, he discovered that a strong palette and pen didn't make a great business operator. One Friday afternoon, he found a pile of collection notices on his manager's desk.

Soon after, Tim was promoted to manage the store and named the experience "the second Captain of the Titanic." The store closed months later but provided several opportunities for him to experiment with different sales strategies and build his mailing list. Tim's new experience helped him land at a well-established wine shop and restaurant, Dexter's. To Tim's dismay, he soon learned Dexter's core strategy was largely competing on price with wines they bought in large volume.

After an educational trip to France with a wine distributor, Tim learned the value of terroir, or natural environment, on wine production and stories of family-run farms. Back at Dexter's, with a greater appreciation for wine and a consultative sales approach, he found himself "selling against the wine of the month." Dexter was not pleased. Tim knew there was a better way to provide superior customer service. His repeat client list grew, and he began his exit plan. He felt he had the tools to start his own wine business; he just needed to iron out the details.

During Labor Day weekend of 1995, Tim was having a lakefront picnic under the shade of a large cypress tree with his wife and infant son. He noticed a for-rent sign across the street on an attractive storefront with large windows covered by a bright forest green awning and enough retail floor space and parking for Tim's dream wine shop. As a bonus, it was on a main road leaving downtown Orlando with constant traffic, so the store acted as a billboard as well.

Tim found an investment partner, locked in a lease, and opened on October 2, 1995. Now he was able to apply his life's work and mailing list to his own vision. He first established key operating tenets: "Always have quality wines and never sacrifice customer service for volume." The experience had to be excellent to drive loyalty. Tim embraced this and taught his team:

"If someone has to wait for your help, put a glass of wine in their hand."

In Tim's first year, he found himself selling wines with high ratings from Robert Parker, a well-known wine critic. Parker's rating system made buying simple for customers.

One Saturday afternoon, as he closed the door after the last customer left, he paused while turning the lock and gazed at the French Burgundy vineyard poster on his wall. He realized something he'd missed while he was so busy trying to run his business for the last year: "If I'm chasing the wine scores, I'm selling the same crap as everybody else and that's not where I want to be."

The new internet model of selling the highest-rated wines at the lowest price was taking hold. Tim knew this was a losing proposition especially in a net consumption state with high shipping costs.[177] When trucks deliver goods to Florida, they often go back empty, so you pay both routes. How could he compete? He had to go back to his roots, with a few modern twists. He created a third tenet to his business: "Sell quality, family-owned wines along with great knowledge and service, making customers loyal to you, not a rating."

Tim knew he needed a well-paid staff, which internet margins made challenging. He concentrated on what he could control: make wine-buying personal and take the time to sell the right wine to customers, creating a pull. Additional twists were to refresh his monthly newsletter with recipes, switch to email, and create a tiered wine club offering.

In 2006 he witnessed the success of the innovative and brash Wine Library TV, from Gary Vaynerchuk, which brought much notoriety. Tim knew he couldn't go that far, but he saw

---

177 "Which States Are Net Producers versus Net Consumers?" *Food Navigator USA*, updated November 3, 2017.

the power of social media and began to leverage Facebook to connect with a younger demographic. This new model was working.

In 2008, the behemoth Total Wine moved two miles from Tim's store. How do you compete with such a massive buyer? He took several trips to various Total Wine locations and studied what they sold, how they sold it, and which distributors they used.

Weeks before Total Wine opened, Tim shared that he "changed distributor alliances, eliminated most overlapping wine labels, and doubled down on our customer service strategy and wine knowledge." He did this by requiring all staff to earn the prestigious Wine and Spirit Education Trust (WSET) level-three certification. Tim built his business through appreciating the value of satisfied customers and continues to evolve this mindset to meet changing customer demands and market conditions.

Tim has insulated himself from Goliath for now and continues to hold tightly to his version of innovation: always have good wines, never sacrifice customer service for volume, and promote family-owned wineries. He now has four locations and generates over four million dollars in annual sales.

With his success, he began teaching entrepreneurship at his alma mater to share his mindset and strategies with others. Tim has demonstrated a persistent ability to effectively understand the market, hold on to his customer centricity, and optimize his operation to achieve superior results in the face of any challenge.

KEEP CALM AND CARRY ON[178]

My first job on Wall Street was as an assistant supporting a sales team. While making copies and sending out literature orders, I inevitably encountered service issues requiring escalation. We had a special segmented service team much like the airlines: platinum, gold, and silver. People on the platinum team were always ready to handle any issue, but one especially stood out: Cher Lindsey. She had a difficult job, serving two customers, the sales team, and their top clients, but always delivered.

It didn't take long to learn that if I had a situation that needed special attention, there was one person to call. Cher understood our business as a sales team and the benefits of helping us navigate a difficult service issue. This clarity and can-do attitude led her to always go out of her way to deliver customer satisfaction.

If there was an impediment to our solution, she would hang up the phone and walk to her manager's office for an answer, to ensure the client always felt confident the situation was handled properly. Occasionally the answer was no, but if that were the case, she professionally offered a full explanation of the rules or policies, so there was no lingering doubt in the client's mind.

Years later, as a veteran external salesperson, I was sitting in my car outside my next appointment. I see "Richard" appear

---

178 Jacopo Prisco, "Keep Calm: The Story behind the UK's Most Famous Poster Design," *CNN Style*, November 1, 2017.

on my caller ID. I cringed, then answered. "We've got a problem!" he barked. I asked a few clarifying questions and knew I needed to call Cher. Richard was the type of client who brought a bittersweet mix of high revenue and ultra-high maintenance.

I connected all three of us on the phone. Cher asked several questions to better comprehend the situation. The answer was a clear "no." He went ballistic, as he often did, and Cher simply and calmly informed him of exactly what the rules were and that we had no flexibility. She had learned over the years that fighting negative energy head on gets you nowhere.

I'll never forget how embarrassed I was to let him treat her that way, but she taught me valuable lessons. Lead with knowledge and a professional demeanor, and in the long run, this will help you build a solid reputation that customers will come back to again and again.

Through Cher, I also discovered that if telling someone the rules isn't satisfactory, they're not a good customer. I terminated my relationship with Richard after this circumstance and used it as motivation to direct my energy toward others to grow and continue to determine what customer excellence truly looks like.

* * *

A customer-centric approach is key, no matter where you do business, what types of products you sell, or how much you rely on technology to operate. As Dollar Shave Club (a subscription-based shaving supply company) has learned, to build an empire against an established dominant player like Gillette, you have to approach customers differently. "We don't respond to situations; we respond to people."[179]

Customers will always want to feel that working with you creates a unique and valuable experience for them, making their lives better. This value can only be delivered after you take the time to discover and fully appreciate their needs.

This can be done with data analytics, as we saw with MD, through leveraging empathy, as we saw with Eric, by building a customer service mindset into your team, as we saw with Tim, or always providing excellent service despite difficult circumstances, as we saw with Cher.

With each approach, listening to and deeply understanding your customer plays a central role. Give them a voice. From there, you can establish policies and strategies to constantly deliver at a high-quality level in a meaningful way. Each of these businesses showcases how a customer-centric mindset of solving problems can be highly impactful to delivering results, and that there is more than one way to execute effectively. In chapter seven, we'll explore how the optimizer mindset is enhanced with a focus on excellence.

---

179 Blake Morgan, "The 10 Most Customer-Obsessed Companies in 2018," *Forbes*, February 15, 2018.

CHAPTER 7

FOCUS ON EXCELLENCE

——

"Perfection is not attainable, but if we chase perfection, we can catch excellence."

—VINCE LOMBARDI

PASSION FOR EXCELLENCE

In 1982, with a seven-year interest-only loan for four hundred thousand dollars, the do-it-yourself (DIY) father-son team of Gus and Todd Anderson fulfilled a lifelong dream and bought a hillside farm in Napa Valley to start a vineyard: Anderson Conn Valley Vineyards (ACVV). They knew there was much to learn to make great wine. Todd joined the Viticultural Technical Group with roughly ninety winemakers. The group spent hours out in the field learning and discussing "everything from prepping bare ground, to getting grapes, to making wine."

Soon, vineyard construction began and Todd and Gus "pounded every stake and strung every wire." Justin Meyer, of highly collectible Silver Oak Cellars, was down the road.

He liked Todd's passion for learning and was happy to be a mentor. He openly shared his winemaking knowledge along with hundreds of budwood vine clones from his finest plot, Bonny's Vineyard. Those clones were planted, treated with exceptional care, and generated the first five acres of ACVV grapes.

That first harvest was in 1983, and the early plan was to sell most of the grapes to other winemakers. The remaining grapes were for the Andersons' maiden vintage. They relished "knocking the berries off the stems by hand" and experimenting with the fermentation process of the grapes. In stark contrast to industry norms, they first used a stainless-steel barrel with oak barrel scraps they hand toasted on their stove, rather than actual oak barrels.

In the early 1980s, grapes were delivered in five-ton gondolas attached to the back of pick-up trucks, bouncing down Highway 29 and Silverado Trail. Todd loved driving those sticky, purple-stained roads with his windows down letting the sweet scent of fresh grapes fill his nostrils.

On a sunny September day, he was delivering grapes to Joe Heitz, founder of the prestigious Heitz Cellars and a "surly old dude." When Todd parked his truck by the Heitz barn, Joe went straight to the grapes for inspection. He found a leaf, held it straight at Todd and shouted, "if I find another leaf, I'm rejecting the next load."

Todd went through the next delivery by hand to ensure that Joe found no leaves. Joe also did a thorough inspection and without a word, went back to his house. Todd recalled that moments later, "Joe marched straight up to me and shoved a bottle in my gut."

"Maybe someday you'll make a wine like this," Joe barked. Todd looked down and saw Martha's Vineyard Cabernet Sauvignon, Heitz's crown jewel. Todd learned that exceptional attention to detail was mandatory to sell grapes to the top winemakers in Napa, down to the leaf.

Each year, the Andersons sold fewer grapes and kept more to hone their own wine making skills while continuing to seek knowledge. They "learned from several Napa 'old-timer' winemakers how they made wine and never stopped experimenting" with their own wine-making process. In 1987, the Andersons released their first commercial vintage which earned critical acclaim.

The DIY guys were happy but continued to tinker. As their experience grew, they optimized the fermentation process by *not* evolving through modern methods. They don't add complexity through additives or machine processes; they use dozens of varieties of existing oak barrel sources and toast levels of the wood to maximize their flavor profiles.

Todd and company also experimented with the brix, or sugar level, at which they harvest grapes. The traditional method of wine making was picking grapes when the brix reached 21 percent of the grape's content. After many trials, the Andersons found a higher brix more appealing. For their 1988 Cabernet Sauvignon vintage, they picked the grapes at a brix level of 25 percent. That wine made the cover of Wine Spectator magazine and "[they] never looked back."[180]

This marked the end of selling grapes and the beginning of solely harvesting grapes for their own production.

Business was going well for this boutique operation, but challenges always lingered. The 1973 "Judgment of Paris" wine competition was won by two California vineyards, Stags Leap and Chateau Montelena, and this "totally changed the game" for California wines.[181] From the "judgment" to 2005, California wine producers grew nearly eight times, to 2,275 in total.[182]

In addition to ever-increasing competition, other challenges were ahead. Gallo wines was consolidating twenty thousand acres of California vineyards to build scale.[183] Southern Glazers liquor distributors bought the ten largest competitors in 2010 to gain market share.[184] And more vineyards sprang up that emphasized vanity over venture, further pressuring

---

180 Augustus Weed, "Napa Winemaker Gus Andrew Anderson Dies at 86," *Wine Spectator*, December 6, 2016.

181 Maria Godoy, "The Judgment of Paris: The Blind Taste Test That Decanted the Wine World," *NPR*, May 24, 2016.

182 Jeff Leve, "Complete Napa Valley California Wine History from Early 1800s to Today," *The Wine Cellar Insider*, accessed May 22, 2020.

183 Bruce Keppel, "Feud Shines Spotlight on Joseph Gallo," *LA Times*, August 10, 1986

184 Stacy Briscoe, "Top 10 U.S. Wine Distributors," *Wines & Vines*, September 2018

pricing.[185] Napa "cabs" were selling for sixty-nine dollars on average in 2019, and a storm was brewing.[186]

"If you're going to require small wineries to only sell through distributors, we're done," Todd shared. His business was 80 percent through distributors at the time. There was a day of reckoning coming for the family-owned vineyards.

Todd knew they had to evolve and began experimenting with personal appearances, growing his brand, and building awareness of the exceptional attention to detail in their wine-making process. He began to understand the "value of connecting the wine to the wine maker and the emotional connection wine enthusiasts developed with favorite labels." However, with only one Todd and forty acres, he knew he had to be strategic and concentrate on premium wines.

One day, Todd met Al Bronstein at Diamond Creek vineyard, the one who sold the first one-hundred-dollar "Napa Cab" in 1982. "People were shocked" by this, so Todd inquired further:[187]

"How do you sell a wine for one hundred dollars?" "You can ask any price you want and sell it once. If the quality

---

185 Paul Sullivan, "Winemaking Lures the Wealthy, but Not with Profits," *NY Times*, May 25, 2012

186 W. Blake Gray, "Napa Pricing Risks Alienating Consumers," Wine-Searcher, January 23, 2020.

187 Bill Ward, "Minnesota Native Changed the Course of Napa Wines," Diamond Creek Vineyards, accessed May 20, 2020.

is there and people like it, they'll come back and you'll have a brand."

Todd learned you need a little audacity with a stellar product and to market your wine in a way that makes people feel value in your brand.

Todd realized being an owner and operator with a winery, he was uniquely positioned to fill a "wine experience" void. In 2000, he quietly created a new ultra-premium craft wine, Ghost Horse, with the tagline, "There's only one lifestyle, the one you want to live." This vineyard produces a few hundred cases each year and has developed a cult-like following with an experience-based club, fine wines, etched glass bottles, and a one-thousand-dollar starting point.[188]

Members of his Ghost Horse allocation club are welcome to join him on adventure trips or have Todd host dinner parties at their homes. For his more typical clients, he developed a four-tier Conn Valley wine club, each well-appointed with unique benefits such as tastings at the vineyard or access to special library wines. You must target your message and pricing appropriately to offer exceptional value at each tier.

This tiered premium strategy is not new, but it can be highly effective. Disney is a master of tiered pricing and experiences of excellence. You can take a family of four to Disneyland and spend $436 for a memorable day.[189] Or, you

---

188 "Our Wines," Ghost Horse Wines, accessed May 19, 2020.

189 "Standard Theme Park Ticket in 2020," Walt Disney World, accessed May 19, 2020.

can purchase a variety of additional VIP packages. The most luxurious adding $5,250 each day for the same family, including seven hours with a personal tour guide who takes you to the front of every line and provides a variety of "behind the scene" moments.[190] The Ghost Horse offerings are all about the experience.

After thirty-eight years in business, Todd shared that Anderson Conn Valley is one of the longest-running owner-operator vineyards in Napa. They have survived a constant stream of challenges and found a way to thrive at every stage of the journey. They've done this through taking the time to understand their client base, making members of all club tiers feel exclusive, not being afraid to experiment with a process or service, and directing energy to produce excellence that keeps people coming back.

INNOVATE FOR EXCELLENCE

"Every generation needs a new revolution."

—THOMAS JEFFERSON

May 1, 1975, marked the beginning of a revolution in the United States. This revolt was barely televised as twenty-four-hour news was still five years away. The leader was not wearing fatigues. He was a well-groomed thirty-eight-year-old in a white pressed shirt and boxy prescription glasses.

---

190 "Disney Private VIP Tours," Walt Disney World, accessed May 19, 2020.

On this day, fixed-rate commissions on stock trades were abolished after being government regulated for nearly 200 years.[191] For the first time ever, investors could price-shop stock trading fees.

Stockbrokers ironically coined the day "Mayday" as they felt heavy distress.[192] It's not often capitalists protest deregulation, but it was not in their favor in this case. To buy or sell a stock prior to Mayday, an investor had to pay five hundred dollars in today's dollars.[193] Today, that transaction can be done for free.

Wall Street was on fire! Innovation was necessary. A dyslexic founder of a fledgling brokerage firm, Charles Schwab, found an answer.[194] He saw this distress call as an opportunity. Sometimes innovation is about responding to disruption. Other times, it's about disrupting yourself, as we saw with our earlier "Problem Solvers." If you make serving your customers your focal point, the answer becomes clearer. On that frightful first day, Schwab took a risk. With clarity of focus, and as others raised commission costs, he took prices lower.[195]

---

191 "May 1st Marks 30th Anniversary of Brokerage Commission Deregulation," *Business Wire*, April 28, 2005.

192 Jason Zweig, "How May Day Remade Wall Street," *A Safe Haven For Investors* (blog), May 1, 2015.

193 Fred Tomczyk, "Lessons from 40 Years of Mayday on Wall Street: Column," *USA Today*, May 1, 2015.

194 Child Mind Institute, "A Conversation with Charles Schwab on Struggling and Succeeding with Dyslexia," March 12, 2019, video, 56:53.

195 "From May Day to Heydays," *Inc.*, October 1, 2019.

Schwab saw the client acquisition opportunity that few others did. He also recognized the power of stock ownership and a low-cost structure, and its impact on one's financial future in contrast to the low percentage of Americans actually investing.[196] I am fortunate to know the power of the stock market firsthand. My parents put one thousand dollars into a mutual fund for me in 1977. Even with a 4 percent commission, the fund has increased over eighty times.

In 1975, the average US household income was $13,779.[197] People needed help for wealth creation, and the 1970s didn't offer many options. Schwab had a client-driven vision to meet that need.[198] That vision was a revolution to make investing accessible to anyone. He was solving a country-wide problem. He opened branches and offered educational seminars, empowering all investors to take ownership of their financial future.[199]

---

196 "Learning from Charles Schwab," *Investment Master Class* (blog), April 10, 2020, accessed September 1, 2020.

197 U.S. Census Bureau, "Household Money Income in 1975 and Selected Social and Economic Characteristics of Households," Publications, Briefs and Reports from Census Bureau Experts, 1975, table A, accessed May 28, 2020.

198 *CNBC*, "Investing Legend Charles Schwab Discusses the Market, His Career and His New Book, 'Invested: Changing Forever the Way Americans Invest,' with CNBC's Bob Pisani," October 7, 2019. video, 18:55

199 "We are Champions of Investors and Those Who Serve Them," Who We Are, Charles Schwab Corporation, accessed June 16, 2020.

Schwab began to experiment with a number of ideas to improve the client experience and invested heavily in technology to support growth, including a twenty-four-hour quote and order service.[200] You have to make it easy for clients to do business with you. Schwab shared, "We were early adopters of technology to make ourselves more efficient."[201]

At this point, Schwab was by far the largest discount brokerage firm in the US.[202] However, there is no guarantee of maintaining success. Growth is not sustainable if clients aren't highly satisfied, trades aren't executed rapidly, and accounts not properly recorded. Schwab always looked to the future and built his company to support growth and, more importantly, to improve the lives of his clients.[203] That is excellence.

What's more remarkable about this period is between 1980 and 1982 the US lived through its worst recession since the Great Depression.[204] The US economy was in serious trouble.

---

200 "Leading an Investor Revolution," Company History 1973–1986, Charles Schwab Corporation, accessed June 15, 2020.

201 Charles Schwab, Interview by David Rubenstein, *The David Rubenstein Show*, February 20, 2020.

202 "Pioneer Discount Broker," *Encyclopedia.com*, updated September 24, 2020.

203 "Our Purpose Drives Our Every Action," Who We Are, Charles Schwab Corporation, accessed June 16, 2020.

204 Tim Sablik, "Recession of 1981–82," *Federal Reserve History*, November 22, 2013.

Yet, Schwab continued to invest in his company to support his client mission.

After a failed attempt to take his company public, he sold to Bank of America in 1983.[205] Some might have quit here or cashed out, but not Schwab. He stayed on and launched a number of new initiatives during this time including The Mutual Fund MarketPlace.[206]

The MarketPlace launched in 1984, when mutual fund assets totaled $371 billion.[207] Only 12 percent of US households owned a mutual fund.[208] MarketPlace was a game changer for investors. Everyone now had simplified access to 140 no-load funds.[209] This was a groundbreaking option for industry as well. Fidelity Investments soon followed.[210] The revolution was continuing.

---

205 John Waggoner, "Icons: Schwab Still Roots for the Small Investor," *USA Today*, April 11, 2013.

206 "1973-1986: Leading an Investor Revolution," Company History, Charles Schwab Corporation, accessed June 15, 2020.

207 Jonathan Burton, "Morningstar Plans $100 Million IPO," *MarketWatch*, May 6, 2004.

208 Federal Reserve Board, Federal Reserve Bulletin, *Mutual Funds and the U.S. Equity Market*, by Eric M. Engen, Andreas Lehnert and Richard Kehoe, (December 2000).

209 "1973-1986: Leading an Investor Revolution," Company History, Charles Schwab Corporation, accessed June 15, 2020.

210 Charles Schwab, Interview by David Rubenstein, *The David Rubenstein Show*, February 20, 2020.

To appreciate how early Schwab was, in 2020, Mutual Fund assets surpassed twenty-five trillion dollars and are owned by 103.9 million Americans.[211]

In 1985, Schwab crossed over one million clients and he wanted independence back.[212] With a loan and a group of investors, Schwab bought the company back within two years.[213] Just before the stock market crash of 1987, he successfully took the company public and watched the stock value drop 60 percent in weeks.[214] It was a scary time. He was able to survive and recover because he built a solid foundation for his clients. They stayed with him.

Accidental Success

Innovation with a focus on your clients can occasionally deliver unexpected and welcome results. Schwab found "accidental success" with ONESOURCE, formerly Market-Place.[215] Schwab's chief compliance officer raised a red flag

---

211 Sean Collins et al., *2020 Investment Company Fact Book: A Review of Trends and Activities in the Investment Company Industry*, Investment Company Institute, 60th Edition, 2020.

212 "1973–1986: Leading an Investor Revolution," Company History, Charles Schwab Corporation, accessed June 15, 2020.

213 Charles Schwab, Interview by David Rubenstein, *The David Rubenstein Show*, February 20, 2020.

214 Ibid.

215 Charles Schwab, *Invested: Changing The Way Americans Invest* (New York: Penguin Random House LLC., 2019), 198–199.

after finding several Schwab clients with power of attorney (POA) over hundreds of accounts.[216] This was highly unusual.

Someone might have POA over one or two family member accounts, but not hundreds of people. Schwab's team learned that independent financial advisors were using ONE-SOURCE as an investment platform for their clients. The advisors charge their own advisory fee to their clients. They then pay Schwab a fee for access to ONESOURCE and use a POA to execute trades on behalf of clients.[217] This "accident" was born out of determination to constantly attempt to better solve client problems. Innovation doesn't always work but allocating time to improve on your mission can increase your chances of success. Assets tripled in the first two years.[218]

Clicking with Investors

In 1994, there were 2,738 websites (and counting), with the additions of Schwab, Amazon, and the Magic 8-Ball.[219] There are almost two billion websites today.[220] Schwab saw an opening to expand investment access further. There were eleven brokerage competitors online at the time.[221] In the

---

216 Ibid.

217 Ibid.

218 Ibid.

219 Adrienne LaFrance, "A Search for the Zombie Websites of 1995," *The Atlantic*, April 21, 2017.

220 "Total Number of Websites," Internet Live Stats, accessed September 9, 2020.

221 Johnson Hur, "History of Online Stock Trading" *Be Businessed*, accessed September 9, 2020.

next six years, Schwab added two million online accounts and soon saw ONESOURCE assets cross one hundred billion dollars.[222] The dedication to delivering for the client paid off once again.

Innovative decisions do not have certain outcomes. Schwab put himself in a vulnerable position to unearth them. Focusing on a sound client mission brings confidence to taking risks no matter what the environment throws at you. In Schwab's case, his focus was delivering excellent access and control of investing to clients.

The dot-com bubble bursting was not far off, forcing layoffs and a reset on Schwab's cost structure.[223] It was painful, but it didn't stop investment in their business. Schwab launched an equity-rating service and began offering tiered services to attract more affluent clients by the end of 2002.[224] As we've seen, tiered services can help gain and maintain new clients. Clients want to feel your services or products address their specific needs.

---

222 "1995–2000: Clicking with Online Investing," Company History, Charles Schwab Corporation, accessed June 15, 2020.

223 "2001–2007: Banking on Added Value," Company History, Charles Schwab Corporation, accessed June 15, 2020.

224 Ibid.

Innovating on Behalf of Clients[225]

As they navigated the Great Recession of 2008, Schwab felt comfortable handing the CEO reigns to Walter W. Bettinger II, the president and chief operating officer, and he picked up where Schwab left off on client-focused excellence.[226]

To put a fine point on the importance of ensuring excellent client experiences, in 2017, Schwab raised the bar once again on the industry and launched a "Satisfaction Guarantee" for any unhappy client.[227] This is a highly unusual policy for any industry, much less financial services, but it aligns with Schwab's mission.

In 2019, Schwab went further and eliminated trading fees on stocks and other securities while continuing to provide a full suite of services for any level investor.[228] Some competitors have grudgingly followed suit, but many have not.

When Schwab makes a decision about the direction of their business, it is always with extreme intent to create an excellent client experience. It is not always clear exactly where a new idea will land, but innovating on behalf of clients is a risk worth taking. The client focus provides guidance to prioritize resources and how to measure success with their initiatives.

---

225 "2008–Now: Innovating on Behalf of Clients," Company History, Charles Schwab Corporation, accessed June 15, 2020.

226 Ibid.

227 Ibid.

228 Ibid.

Reflecting on his career, Charles Schwab shared, "Have a team of people around you that you honor. You can do so many more things with brilliance around you."[229] Schwab and his team work relentlessly to exceed expectations and set new standards for the industry. The firm now holds the largest client asset pool of any publicly traded financial services firm in the US, at over four trillion dollars, and the revolution is not over.[230]

OPTIMIZING TO MAXIMIZE CLIENT EXPERIENCE

Starting my career in 1996 in the asset management business in NYC, my state school pedigree felt limited compared to my peers, so I set out with a simple strategy: outwork everyone as best as I can and consistently seek greater responsibility. Good weather or bad, I often found myself hearing the sound of dozens of lights turning on as I flipped the ten switches that lit up my department in a large open corner of the thirty-third floor of 2 World Trade Center.

In the coming years, this strategy and a little luck earned me a few promotions, and it felt as though things were improving. However, I quickly discovered that as you move up in the ranks, the competition only grows. Simply working harder wasn't enough. I needed to find a better path, and it included the insight of others.

---

229 Charles Schwab, Interview by David Rubenstein, *The David Rubenstein Show*, February 20, 2020.

230 "Our Results Speak for Themselves," Who We Are, Charles Schwab Corporation, accessed June 16, 2020.

Thanks to the guidance of several colleagues, I landed a coveted external sales position in January of 2003. I continued to dig deeply into my strategy and work harder. The region had been under-served for a variety of reasons and it gave me the luxury of showing rather quick improvement that lasted a number of years.

After four full years in the position, I was fortunate enough to win the top award given to a member of my team. I was feeling pretty good. It was now January of 2007. I had no clue the Great Recession was on the horizon, but I had a shiny new trophy on my bookshelf that told me everything I was doing was enough.

The 2008 recession cut our business by roughly 40 percent, but we found a way to survive. When your revenue is largely based on your assets under management and the S&P 500 is down 38 percent, it hurts.[231] We managed this disaster as an organization by being in a decent financial position before the downturn and by taking a very transparent approach with our clients as to the missteps we made and how we would avoid them in the future. This strategy worked well, and my results continued to be strong relative to my peers.

Over the next couple of years, my results drifted closer to average. I consistently made excuses as to why, to make myself feel better. At our annual kick off meeting during

---

231 "Vanguard 500 Index Fund Investor Shares," *Yahoo Finance*, accessed August 31, 2020.

the award ceremony, I sat anxiously awaiting my name to be called, but that moment never came.

I began to feel a sweat break over me as I realized I wasn't even in the running for the award and I was really disappointed in myself for growing so comfortable in my role.

"The worst lies are those we tell ourselves."

–RICHARD BACH

I turned to a colleague, Tim, sitting next to me and said, "I have to get my business turned around."

After all the awards were handed out, I made a direct line to Ian, the top award winner that year. After offering my congratulations, I asked, "Did you do anything differently to drive such solid results this year?" He replied, "Yes, I surveyed my top clients to better understand the effectiveness of our business relationship and how I could improve it."

His answer was so simple, yet incredibly powerful and innovative for 2011 in the industry. He made himself vulnerable and solicited direct feedback from his clients, knowing his ego was fully at risk. With these new insights, he modified his business plan, improved relationships across his client base and sales took off.

I asked him to email me his survey as soon as possible, made some minor edits and began my own journey of discovery. Asking clients what they think of you and how you operate can be a humbling exercise. Words matter in these conversations, and I asked Ian for further guidance on how to introduce these conversations. He obliged.

With proper framing, this exercise gave me the most valuable insight I had ever found to grow my business. When you ask someone for feedback about yourself, based on the high level of respect you have for how they handle themselves, it's a powerful exercise in relationship and trust building. More importantly, it gives you a glimpse of your "brand" and how they view you.

There were some painful moments for sure. I asked one long-time client, Mike, a question I thought for sure opened the door to nothing more than flattery.

"What do you like best about working with my company?" I asked with a confident grin, waiting for the compliments. "You guys have great products," he replied.

That hurt. As I drove away from that meeting, I realized I had much work ahead to build my brand with my clients and this survey provided an excellent starting point. I also realized, had I never put myself in that vulnerable place, I never would have found this level of truth.

There were positives from this exercise. Direct client insight left no doubt where they found real value in our relationship and that helped me optimize my business plan to better address their true needs. It was a real-time start, stop, continue exercise for delivering excellence to my clients.

With a refined approach to engaging clients, the next two years my business experienced strong growth, and I found myself with another award and a promotion into leadership.

As a new leader to those who were recently my peers, I was in a bit of an awkward position with some team members. How do I connect with them now as their boss? I found leveraging this innovative strategy of feedback and action with my team was equally powerful for building trust, growing our business, and creating a culture of innovation.

During our years together, enabling and empowering team members to innovate became contagious, and we began to raise the bar on ourselves. My top innovators always found better ways to execute their business plan, but over time, each team member was bringing forward innovative ideas, and that's when I knew I was on to something.

* * *

Excellence is the result of working to constantly deliver exceptional value. You may not always know the impact of a new idea, but if done with a goal of elevating your product or service for your customers, you increase your chances of success.

To offer true value, you must be vulnerable enough to seek honest feedback from customers and employees, aware enough to know there are always further problems to be solved, use empathy to understand your customers' needs, and have a focus to always want to deliver more.

Now that we have explored the principles of the optimizer, in chapter eight we will zero-in on how to help your team adopt this mindset.

PART 3

BUILDING AND LEADING A CULTURE OF OPTIMIZATION

CHAPTER 8

SHIFTING THE MINDSET

OLD HABITS ARE HARD TO BREAK

In 2020, 1.4 trillion digital photos are expected to be taken, 91 percent of them on smartphones.[232] If one took a photo every second, it would take 45,544 years, and a callous thumb, to match the world's effort.[233] My parents still have a pile of hardcover analog photo albums in their basement, filled with years of family memories caught on actual 35mm print film. There was no deleting or editing, just what that moment in time captured.

When you open these albums and peel back the crinkly clear cellophane sheet covering each page, you'll find three things on the back of each photo. The date the photo was taken, a sticky residue from the book page to hold the photo in place, and a Kodak label.

---

232 David Carrington, "How Many Photos Will Be Taken in 2020?" Inspiration/Tech Today, January 10, 2020.

233 Ibid.

Kodak dominated the film industry for decades with the slogan they launched with their first camera in 1888: "You push the button, we do the rest."[234] George Eastman invented Kodak cameras after struggling to haul a microwave-sized version on vacation as a young adult.[235] Kodak spent decades improving and simplifying the act of taking photos with the goal "to make the camera as convenient as the pencil."[236]

Around 1976, Kodak had a 90 percent market share in film sales and 85 percent in cameras.[237] That year, they came up with a brilliant idea to continue to push innovation and optimize their imaging business further. They invented the first digital camera but put little effort behind it, given their dominance in film.[238] By 1988, they employed 145,000 people worldwide and were top twenty-five in revenue on the Fortune 500 list, not far behind Procter & Gamble.[239]

They came back to the digital idea in 1994 in a joint venture with a newer computer company named Apple, creating a

234 Bernard Weisberger, "You Press the Button, We Do the Rest," *American Heritage*, October 1972.

235 Ibid.

236 Andrew Hudson, "The Rise & Fall of Kodak: A Brief History of The Eastman Kodak Company, 1880 to 2012," *Photosecrets*, August 29, 2012.

237 Ibid.

238 John Aldred, "The World's First Digital Camera, Introduced by the Man Who Invented It," *DIY Photography*, August 2, 2016.

239 "Fortune 500: A Database of 50 Years of Fortune's List of America's Largest Corporations," *Fortune*, accessed August 31, 2020.

basic seventy-five-dollar low-resolution camera.[240] Kodak was so concerned with cannibalizing their film business, they left their name entirely absent from the Apple Quick-Take 100.[241] A year later, they launched the first full-featured digital camera priced under one thousand dollars.[242] They felt they could maintain relevance in the film business as customers could use one of their fifty-five thousand world-wide self-serve print-and-edit kiosks to convert digital images to film.[243] Kodak determined film was the solution but didn't focus on the ease of use problem that customers wanted solved.

Between 1999 and 2011, film sales plummeted from eight hundred million rolls of film per year to below one hundred thousand, while Kodak made eighteen acquisitions of other firms.[244] In 2019, Kodak generated $116 million in profits with five thousand employees, roughly 90 percent below its 1996 peak.[245] In contrast to Kodak's aversion to embracing digital, Apple has delivered markedly different results and is now the second most profitable company in the world, generating fifty-nine billion dollars in profit with

240 Robert Grant, *Contemporary Strategy Analysis*, 8th edition (United King-dom: John Wiley & Sons Ltd, 2013), 572.

241 Stewart Wolpin, "20 Years Ago, Apple and Kodak Launched the Digital Camera Revolution," *Mashable*, June 21, 2014.

242 Grant, *Contemporary Strategy Analysis*.

243 Ibid.

244 Ibid.

245 "Kodak Reports Full-Year 2019 Financial Results," *AP News*, March 17, 2020.

137,000 employees.[246] Kodak was a world leader in driving innovation and optimizing the camera and film for millions, but they wouldn't pivot away from their non-digital legacy.[247]

With a strong balance sheet, entering this period of change allowed them the privilege and ability to forgo embracing the business in which they actually competed. Kodak never fully shifted their mindset to functioning in a purely digital manner to discover what that model would look like. They were in the image business, not the film business, and the market soon made them aware of their misguided grip on the past.

Unfortunately for Kodak, customers loved the simplicity of taking digital photos more than their old crinkly paged photo albums, and Kodak finally admitted defeat with film and began to rebuild in 2011.[248]

WHAT IS THE OPTIMIZER MINDSET?

We know that innovation brings change and opens the door to fear, loss, uncertainty, and shame. We also know standing still is not a path to success. We can't simply ignore emotions. We need to embrace them and learn.

---

246 "Apple: Number of Employees 2006-2020 | Aapl," *Macrotrends*, accessed April 22, 2020.

247 Grant, *Contemporary Strategy Analysis*.

248 Ibid.

As Harvard professor Calestous Juma said, "Fear is essential with change, it leads us to questioning, exploring, and discovering what could go wrong."[249] This is why the incremental approach is a key element to driving change with an ongoing feedback loop. Small steps help to dampen the likely emotional reaction to change and feedback drives team engagement.

Your team needs to be actively involved in decisions. They will find flaws in the business plan if they're empowered to do so. Welcoming them to planning discussions will help reveal the issues, but the invite needs proper framing. This isn't to discover why someone's idea is bad. It's asking, "How can our team better solve a problem to deliver something excellent for our customers?"

Open your team to this mindset of consistently allocating time to finding opportunities to be more efficient and effective in their role and in your business. Allow them to be curious. The closer they are to your customer, the better they can provide insight to unearth better paths forward for your business. Every issue can't be solved simultaneously.

As a leader, it's about creating a team of serial optimizers while balancing change efforts with a larger vision of the organization. This requires work by the leader but shouldn't be done alone; your team needs to be engaged in the journey

---

249 Calestous Juma, "Resistance is Futile," interview by Ramtin Arablouei and Rund Abdelfatah, *Throughline*, NPR, April 25, 2019, audio, 37:01.

to increase your chances of success. As a veteran portfolio manager put it:

> ## "If you're going to be innovative, you have to have a high level of engagement from your team to make improvements."
>
> —MICHELLE BORRE

To make this work, you and your team need to be able to answer several questions:

- What business are we in?
- What's our mission?
- How will we get there?
- Why should I care?
- Will this actually work?
- How can I best contribute?
- What does progress look like for me?

Getting these questions answered, even reasonably well, ultimately increases your team's chances to deliver better results for your business and growing team member engagement in the process. Your best team members embrace optimization on their own, but few will do so without proper motivation. How do leaders instill a culture where team members live with this mindset? By building a strategy to enable, empower, and sustain your team to do so.

SO WHY BOTHER WITH OPTIMIZATION?

Disruption is all around us and executing it well within a changing framework is difficult. Ideas are easy to come up with, making them awesome is the hard work. Therefore, we need to generate ideas, flesh them out with the team, determine if they can be relevant, and discover how to make them better so we can create the next light bulb.

No matter your industry, someone is trying to take your market share, and yet, overheard in your company is, "We're fine, we don't need to change." It's incredible to think George Eastman built a product to radically improve the early camera and then he himself was displaced by the digital era and smartphones. Worse yet, it happened while Kodak had a front-row seat.

You need to manage your business for today, but if you aren't allocating resources to finding and committing to opportunities to understand and evolve your business, your margins will come under pressure, as Kodak experienced. However, no one person can solve all a company's issues, therefore you need to engage the entire team in the planning process and create benchmarks to measure.

> *The change you need won't happen by chance.*

After working on building a culture of optimizers with a sales team, I found them increasing activities of learning together. They were teaching each other and innovating, often without prompting, and delivering solid results. A newer and younger team member, James, started out running fast and hard, as many have (including myself).

In his early months, he took just about every meeting he could get, working twelve-plus hours each day, and quickly learned that some clients are willing to waste your time. He felt it would toughen him up enough to make the task easier in the future. He was a bit right. But could he work smarter?

What really changed the trajectory of his business and complemented his tenacity was mentoring from his peers on how to best leverage the resources we had at our disposal. More importantly, his teammates were happy to offer their guidance.

The team had an inclination to collaborate, but we spent time building a process to consistently bring the best ideas forward and help the entire group deepen relationships amongst each other, making collaboration more organic. The environment we created fostered mentorship and idea-sharing from everyone. It's possible to be mentored by a peer, even as a veteran, if you're willing to learn. In this case, James was mentored by several veterans and was able to accelerate his learning curve and achieve the top growth rate on the team for his first two years.

WHAT CAN OPTIMIZERS DO FOR YOU?

Optimizers believe they will succeed and are free to create. They are not worried about keeping their jobs, they're worried about delivering excellence.

This is critical to why they drive results. This is a unique group that has growth and innovation built into their DNA. If you can multiply their mindset across the team, you'll raise the bar. This mindset knows standing still is really moving backwards and is not an option. These natural optimizers are a solid starting point for determining who your informal team leaders are if you aren't already aware.

Their most obvious traits are always trying to improve and learn from every set-back. Work with this group and challenge them to grow further. They are the most difficult group to try to lift, but it is worth it. Don't assume because they deliver strong results, they can't get better and don't want you to help them grow. Publicize their journey, and you'll see their mindset continue to grow and spread across your team. It will become contagious and each team member will find new highs, worry less about the lows, and improve performance.

Serial Optimizer at Work

Paul grew up a military brat, the son of a top Air Force pilot, with a far greater passion for sports than academics. His father joined the Air Force right after high school, as officers didn't need college degrees at the time. Paul's father had little fear when he was in the cockpit. His mother stayed at home, and his father finished college in his thirties. They were good people but didn't have experience with money or the business world and provided Paul with limited educational or career guidance along the way.

Paul sensed there was more to life and found himself awestruck in high school by a pipe-smoking English teacher with a PhD. This teacher, Dr. Geiss, "made literature come alive better than any movie." Paul had seen how the doctor captivated students with his stories. Paul was inspired by this gifted orator, and one day after class he asked, "How can I learn to talk like you?"

The doctor directed Paul to Winston Churchill's six-volume series on World War II as one of the greatest models for storytelling to date. Paul spent the next two years reading every page and found his vocabulary growing rapidly as well as his ability to tell stories that drew listeners in. He loved this new skill and began to wonder how it could be applied to his life.

Impressed by Dr. Geiss, Paul attended the University of Arizona to become a teacher. After a year of teaching and being on his own, he felt he wanted a better financial life and began a new career search. He spent his first summer off from school job searching. It was 1978 and unemployment in the US was 6 percent and headed to over 10 percent in the next few years, versus a historical rate of roughly 4 percent.[250]

He spent hours at the local library "combing through the Dun & Bradstreet reference books" learning about different companies and industries. He felt his story telling would serve him well in sales and applied for dozens of positions, only to find his lack of experience closing every door.

---

250 Kimberly Amadeo and Somer G. Anderson, "Unemployment Rate by Year since 1929 Compared to Inflation and GDP: U.S. Unemployment Rate History," *The Balance*, Updated August 7, 2020.

As luck would have it, his father had a friend at the largest retailer in the country at the time, Sears Roebuck. Paul was able to land a spot in their leadership development program, "Selling carpet and drapes."

As the months went on, Paul found fewer customers in search of upgrading their homes as high unemployment persisted and interest rates to finance an upgrade were roughly 16 percent.[251] One day, searching the back-office file cabinet, he found a large folder filled with contact information on previous Sears customers. He briskly walked over to a colleague and exclaimed, "I've found an opportunity for us. Leads!" The two marched straight into their manager's office to share the great news.

"We found leads to call on!"

"This is Sears. We don't call people, they come to us."

Paul quit shortly after, knowing his upside was limited to inbound customers.

Now he was on a mission. He had a little experience under his belt and found a sales position with Principal Financial Group. He found an organization that rewarded motivated employees for thinking differently and bringing in new business. He simply took the time to understand his clients and

---

251 "Consumer Credit Outstanding and Finance Rates, 1980 to 2000," *Infoplease*, accessed March 25, 2020.

why they wanted insurance. "It's not because they want to die. They want peace of mind."

Paul leveraged his storytelling to help potential customers connect with how insurance was helping them sleep better by "creating a comprehensive protection plan for their families." His sales grew like wildfire and he was soon one of the top two salesmen in the company. The leadership team liked his approach and asked him to be a manager and build a team. Before long, his team was leading the company in sales, but Paul felt he could do more. He had seen the power of understanding client issues and shared how "treating the patient and not the disease" was the true secret to financial planning.

With a solid track record, he went back to the larger firms that originally turned him down and found a spot at Merrill Lynch. He took a pay cut to get there but recognized the value of marrying his financial planning skills with a brokerage powerhouse. After months of training he found a Welcome Wagon representative selling leads in the office conference room to young brokers and signed up for an affluent retirement community.

After the first set of leads came to Paul, he realized with a few more questions asked by Welcome Wagon, he could build better rapport and profile prospects much more effectively. He called the Welcome Wagon person and asked, "Would you add a few more questions to the profiles if I paid another dollar per lead?" They obliged and his business took off once again, now at a large firm.

He learned that getting to know prospects before they met helped him better relate to their situation and create clearer paths to teaching them to understand the value of financial planning. He was able to not just sell insurance, but take them on as full-service financial advisory clients, bringing their entire wealth in, not just one account. He was again at the top of his class in results.

Soon, Paul found himself promoted to a manager spot in Los Angeles. He spent the first few weeks on a listening tour, spending time with each new team member. He wanted to ensure he knew what was on their minds what problems needed solving. Experience taught him that understanding his team's needs and goals was as powerful, if not more, than understanding clients. After meeting with several new team members, Paul invited the top advisor in the office to lunch, but he declined.

The next day, Paul walked into his office and asked, "Why does Michael Jordan need Phil Jackson?" To which the advisor looked up from his paperwork, confused, and asked, "What?" Paul went on, "Michael Jordan is in the game and can't see what's going on around him from a broader context. Phil is there to help Michael better execute in the midst of chaos."

Sometimes you have to be a bit audacious. Lunch was now scheduled, and their relationship grew. Months later, Merrill launched Financial Foundations, a financial planning tool. Paul knew this would work and spent months teaching the advisors how to articulate and leverage the plan, and ultimately build more sustainable advisory businesses and increase clients' chances of hitting their goals. Six months after the launch of the new tool, Paul's branch became the number one for financial planning in the country.

Back to His Roots

After ten years in LA, he wanted to move back to Dallas, where he had enjoyed time in his youth. He appreciated the leadership philosophy he had learned about at Smith Barney and called the local leader in Dallas for an informational interview. The leader couldn't believe he wanted to give up what he built in LA and didn't have a manager spot at the time. However, he was able to offer him a trainer position. Paul accepted.

He packaged up his life's work and learnings as an advisor and leader and built a training program with a small team at his new firm. After hosting several training sessions, he realized his calling was, in fact, teaching and solving every challenge. He enjoyed helping others to become better leaders and business operators. His optimizer mindset helped him recognize that a career shift was needed in order to find a way to work within his passion. This role allowed him to help clients live better lives, help advisors do better work, and find great fulfillment for himself.

In 2011, Paul saw a unique opportunity to bring the coaching model to the asset management industry. He recognized the value in consultative sales and developing business leaders, which were applicable there as well. He slowly built a team, developed coaching content, and upskilled an army of sales-people that consistently delivered strong results. This success landed him as the director of consultative sales at one of the top ten largest asset managers in the world, leading a new business team to execute arguably the most important initiative for the firm and staying relevant.

Paul exhibits the optimizer mindset. If you continue to improve your skills, consistently ask, "What's a better way to solve this problem?" and take the time to develop a process to understand your employees or clients, you're on the right track. This allows you the power to effectively "treat the patient, not the disease," as he puts it.

* * *

How do you build a culture of optimizers?

It's done through a process! You must enable, empower, and sustain this effort. It won't happen on its own. Design a systematic plan that engages every team member in the journey to consistently elevate and share their skillset. Help them discover a reason to be front-and-center with their peers and give them the stage. I call this lifting the curve, as in the talent curve.

These are keys to unlocking an optimizer culture.

You need to take the time to understand your team members on a personal level and their motivations in order to develop their buy-in of the culture you're building. Additionally, it needs to be clear to all that as innovation progresses, failure and learning will be part of the experience. Nothing is risk-free.

Creating a culture of optimizers has the power to change the trajectory of your business, but it is no simple task; it's a process. The last three chapters of this book will outline the steps to build and lead such a team and embed this new mindset into all. None of this is possible without your team members trusting you; therefore, let's move the discussion there next.

CHAPTER 9

ENABLE THE OPTIMIZER

BUILDING TRUST

"Teamwork begins by building trust. And the only way to do that is to overcome our need for invulnerability."

—PATRICK LENCIONI

Safety First

Today we live in the Fourth Industrial Revolution which is characterized by rapid integration of technologies in our daily work.[252] The first through third revolutions were about mechanization, mass production, and automation respectively.[253] This new revolution has brought challenges that require constantly evolving both soft and hard skills. Yet,

---

252 Klaus Schwab, "The Fourth Industrial Revolution: What It Means, How to Respond," *World Economic Forum*, January 14, 2016.

253 Ibid.

a CEO survey by PricewaterhouseCoopers, a consultancy firm, shows only 18 percent of organizations feel they've made "significant progress" with up-skilling programs, while 10 percent have made none.[254] There is much work to be done.

You're in leadership because you've excelled in prior roles and convinced a firm that you were the clear choice to move ahead, or you started the business. As a leader, your responsibilities catapult relentlessly forward, and it's no longer just about you. Whether at ten weeks or ten years, growing your teams' capabilities is critical to maintaining relevance.

During this evolution, you'll need enormous buy-in from your team, and the most sustainable way to get them on that bus is through trust. There is no way for any one leader to solve every problem. You need to engage others in the journey and help them grow. To do this, you have to exhibit vulnerability as you invite team members into decision making and problem solving. You must be empathetic to the challenges everyone faces in the learning curve.

Innovation through optimization is pivotal to building durable success in any organization. However, building trust is necessary to driving that change. It is miles from easy to establish, and the steps will occasionally leave you unnerved. Trust creates a safe environment for risk taking, enabling

---

254 Carol Stubbings and Bhushan Sethi, "Talent Trends 2020: Upskilling: Building Confidence in an Uncertain World," *PwC CEO Survey*, accessed June 15, 2020.

employees to join the growth journey and not just watch from a distance.

Trust Enables Growth

After one of my sales team members departed the firm in 2016, I had a decision to make. The region was one of the smallest in the country. I could have replaced them with a new hire but given the slow-down our business was experiencing, I felt we needed a longer-term solution.

I requested permission to eliminate the sales region and reallocate the geography to adjacent team members, but I needed to work on the details. I poured through the data and explored several options. No matter what, this decision was going to have a significant lifestyle impact on one of my most tenured team members, requiring him to spend far more time on overnight trips. It was evident he was not going to be enthusiastic about any big change, but I needed to find a way to make it work, to make it feel like a safe choice. What would you do?

"Dave, I'm thinking about not replacing Jeff, and reallocating his region."

"Okay, what are you considering?"

"Dave, you've been around here a long time and understand this geography far better than I do. I'd really like your views on how you think we could make this work best."

"What?" he said.

"I'd like to hear your thoughts on how I should think about this change."

"Wow! Can you give me a few days to come up with a plan?"

"Sure. Thanks for your help."

This decision was quite far along, but given his experience and thoughtfulness, I wanted to gain his insights, as I was sure he'd find something I'd overlooked. We met that Friday at a Starbucks to go through his best-case scenario. His ideas overlapped about 80 percent with my existing proposal.

Both of our plans included a significant increase to his budget and adding another member to his team. Additionally, I made further changes to adjacent sales regions to make his one of the largest in the country. Dave was a little disappointed not getting exactly what he proposed, but at the same time he relished being part of the process.

The changes were now largely his, not mine. He had ownership. It wasn't a perfect transition; that never happens. However, he was energized by the engagement and embraced the moment. Inviting him into the decision made him feel safe to speak up, drew out his creativity, and drove adoption. He spent the next two years improving his results and found himself promoted.

WHY HAVE SUCH A DILEMMA WITH TRUST?

"A lack of trust is the biggest expense in organizations."
—DAVID HORSAGER, CEO OF TRUST EDGE
LEADERSHIP INSTITUTE.

It's much easier to manage activity than lead successfully, and it's easier to keep information hidden than to share it openly. This can feel like power. It's not. An activity-based nontransparent culture paves the shortest road to mediocrity. Before you know it, "checking boxes" will become more important to your team than driving results. As the insight of one of your best sources of creativity goes ignored, you slowly erode their self-esteem, and the idea-waterfall slows to a drip. Now your relationship grows damaged, and you can forget about building trust.

A firm that lacks transparency misses the mark on trust, creating a culture of fear and apprehension. Without trust, fearful employees will work to protect their seats and leave growth for others to solve. You'll know this has happened when innovators grow quiet at meetings and refresh their LinkedIn profiles, seeking new opportunities. Employee turnover is detrimental to any team, for morale and cost.

WHAT CAN TRUST DO FOR YOU?

Gallup estimates that 70 percent of variance in employee engagement is driven by managers.[255] When you trust your manager, the results are clear. Employees feel empowered, initiatives are adopted more quickly, mistakes by leaders are given the benefit of the doubt, and team members are twice as likely to stay with the company.[256]

According to the consultancy Great Place to Work, they've found *Fortune*'s 100 Best Companies to Work For have delivered stock returns of nearly three-times greater than the market average.[257] The standard for a "great place to work" is a high ranking on their "Trust Index Survey."[258] With a foundation anchored in trust, you enable innovation and drive results.

According to Zenger and Folkman, the key elements of trust are: Positive Relationships, Good Judgement/Expertise, and Consistency.[259] What does this mean?

---

255 Randall J. Beck and Jim Harter, "Why Great Managers Are So Rare," *Gallup Workplace Business Journal*, accessed June 17, 2020.

256 Jim Harter, "Why Some Leaders Have Their Employees' Trust, and Some Don't," *Gallup Workplace*, June 13, 2019.

257 Julie Musilek, "Why Trust Beats Employee Engagement," (blog), *Great Place To Work*, July 31, 2019.

258 "The definition of a Great Workplace," *Great Place to Work*, accessed May 8, 2020.

259 Jack Zenger and Joseph Folkman, "The 3 Elements of Trust," *Harvard Business Review*, February 5, 2019.

> *Know your team members and their motivations; this isn't a one-time event.*

Take time to consider the next steps for your business and utilize team input where appropriate. Reflect on and inquire about your internal brand.

Finally, lead by example: exhibit behaviors that create a road map to success, never stop educating yourself, deliver on what you say, and be transparent along the journey with the plan.

Be vulnerable and let the team know you want and need their input, as no one can make a perfect plan.

When your team trusts you, your views, and your relationship, you unleash their creative potential and enable them to reach new highs rather than work to avoid lows.

HOW DO YOU BUILD TRUST AND ENABLE YOUR TEAM TO GROW?

"Building trust is a process. Trust results from consistent and predictable interaction over time."

—BARBARA M. WHITE, FIRST FEMALE TO GAIN
AMBASSADORIAL RANK IN THE UNITED NATIONS

Get Personal

Building trust does not happen with one email or paying someone a compliment. It takes time and effort and is built by your actions, following your words. Your team needs to know what kind of person you are and what to expect from you in a variety of business climates.

Knowing each team member personally is the starting point to trust. They have to know you care and support them in their effort and that you know both their personal and professional situation. This will accelerate the building of trust and, more importantly, the understanding of what truly motivates them to take action.

At some point, you'll be offering advice or coaching on how they can improve on something. If they don't believe you know them, that conversation will take a long time to resonate, or it may never. Just because you're their boss and said something doesn't mean they will jump right in, even with trust. So, without trust, you're simply delaying adoption or eliminating the chance of truly getting buy-in.

Do you need questions here for a starting point?

It's best to begin work with a new team by taking a listening tour, but it's never too late to use this strategy. Let this tour be a part of your relationship-building effort. A mindset shift here is to think of your employees as clients. How will you keep them happy, retained, and helping you to grow your business? Getting to know them on a personal level will open doors for this to work. Most people with children love to share stories about them. If you don't know your employee has children, you'll never understand the degree to which their family impacts their level of motivation.

Other questions to help you get started or to grow your relationship:

- What made you get into this industry?
- Tell me about yourself.
- Who's been a great mentor in your career and why?
- What motivates you?
- Where do you like to vacation? Why?

The key here is to truly be curious as you dig deeper, and then capture these insights in writing. This will give you opportunities to better connect with your team members in the future.

At a semi-annual conference, one of my team members was celebrating a landmark birthday. As a leader with the firm, I had a suite reserved for me. Given it was his birthday, I borrowed an idea from our CEO, Arthur Steinmetz. I secretly traded rooms with the birthday boy and had a selection of his favorite craft beers and a birthday cake waiting for him when he arrived with a personalized note. After he checked into his room, he sent me a text and asked me to stop by. He gave me a quick tour of his suite, showed me the gift basket, and told me "no one had ever done anything so thoughtful in his career."

> *Financial rewards are always nice, but showing them you care and are listening to them is priceless.*

Let Them Speak...and Listen

Gaining feedback from your team can be done more than one way, as we saw with The Motley Fool, and is absolutely critical to building trust. It's not just your team that needs to be curious, but also their leader. You need to be curious about your business and what's on the minds of your team.

Before you think about engaging your team, consider this exercise from Dr. Tomas Chamorro-Premuzic. Open Google and type "my manager is..." and see what appears.[260] Spoiler alert: none of it is positive. Do any sound like you?

Take time to reflect on the seven autocompletes that appear and fill in the blank yourself. This is a view of your internal brand and leadership style. When considering your brand, do these emotionally intelligent descriptors come to mind: trustworthy, empathetic, considerate, vulnerable, caring, and knowledgeable? How about "leader," "manager," or "boss?" Or does the Google search feel more on point?

"Your brand is what other people say about you when you're not in the room."

—JEFF BEZOS, AMAZON CEO.

---

260 Tomas Chamorro-Premuzic, *Why Do So Many Incompetent Men Become Leaders?: (And How to Fix It)* (Boston: Harvard Business Review Press, 2019), 1.

> *Having a strong handle on your brand is paramount to building trusting relationships.*

Take time to reflect on what you believe your personal brand is with your team and embrace this scary idea at least once each year. Solicit feedback from your team members directly, either face-to-face or by email, and act on it if you can. If you can't take action now, share why, thank them for their insight, and keep an "idea file," noting the author for future use. Every idea your team comes up with won't be viable, but you can keep them in a creative mode and hand-pick the best ideas to carry forward, large or small.

The Google search exercise can help you frame your questions, or you can start here:

- How have I been helpful in your career or role?
- How could I be more helpful?
- How could our team work more effectively toward our goals?
- How clear are our business objectives?
- What could I be doing better as our team leader?

> *Be prepared for answers you may not want to hear...This is how you grow. Great leaders do this regularly, and it gets easier over time.*

The first time you ask these, the quality of answers will have a high correlation to that person's perception of the relationship they have with you, a prior manager, or their comfort in job security. In feedback discussions, you need to capture insights, decide what to measure, and learn how it's impacting your team. As you take action from feedback, announce what you're doing with the team.

Give Credit Where Credit is Due

About one year into a leadership role, I sensed the team wasn't engaged enough in communicating and idea sharing. I asked a tenured team member, Bryan:

"How can we better communicate as a remote team?"

"Cut the number of conference calls we do!"

His response came so quickly, I wondered if he'd been waiting for this question his entire career. I quickly evaluated the entire year of calls and recognized we could easily eliminate almost 20 percent of them, largely by canceling calls that fell on holidays or internal conference weeks. I canceled call invites and announced a new pilot call schedule based on Bryan's feedback. This vulnerable act of asking for his advice quickly made him a supporter. Sometimes less is more when it comes to communicating. With fewer calls, engagement grew with less prompting from me.

At the end of the year, I asked the team, "Should we bring the calls back?" The silence was deafening. This didn't preclude me from having occasional one-off calls. It did liberate several mornings on my team's calendars, and, more importantly, let them know we were in this together. This simple act was a turning point. The team took notice and new ideas began to appear from across the group.

Small changes that elevate a team member can have outsized results. The bar to build engagement on your team is lower than you think. A full 25 percent of employees in the US feel outright ignored by their manager.[261] Consistently giving your team a voice is powerful for building trust.

As a feedback loop becomes part of the process and you broadcast the changes, you'll find:

Increased value in feedback and change you're implementing.Personal brand growth as a trusted advisor and future change easier to launch.

Mission engagement takes a leap forward. Is the mission clear? Ask!

As my old manager Dave Robertson once said, "Good begets good." Create a positive experience for team member contributions, promote the idea, and this will become contagious.

---

261 Susan Sorenson, "How Employees' Strengths Make Your Company Stronger," *Gallup Workplace Business Journal*, accessed June 12, 2020.

Transparency

"The best thing any leader can do to earn trust is facilitate transparency."

–JEFF YURCISIN, ZULILY PRESIDENT/CEO[262]

Feedback and transparency go hand in hand.

David Gardner, Co-Founder of The Motley Fool (TMF) has creative ideas on sharing information. The company hosts biannual "campfire story" sessions. The term "campfire" is used very explicitly to set the tone for storytelling, not charts and graphs. They have veteran employees tell the history of the company, challenges they've faced, how they navigated them, and the outcome. Employees don't like to hear about layoffs and cost cutting, but through these stories "they learn about the values of the company and gain a better understanding of how the next challenge will be addressed."

In addition to sharing stories, TMF regularly shares data on how the company is performing financially. They have scheduled "all hands" open-forum Q&A sessions throughout the year. These meetings capture a real-time sense of what's on people's minds, and they invite employees to challenge ideas.

As Kara Chambers, VP of People Insights, shared, "We are a company of investors and our leaders are accountable to

---

262 Lisa Evans, "How to Build a Culture of Trust in Your Company," *Fast Company*, December 11, 2018.

employees who are shareholders. People are not shy about sharing their views on internal decisions." Keep in mind these employees are professionals that TMF hired because they're amazing at analyzing other companies on their performance and decisions they've made.

They scrutinize leadership decisions at TMF just as they would for a company's stock they are considering recommending for their clients to buy. This is tight rope walking at best, but the way they've embraced this unique challenge with total transparency has helped them build an extraordinary business.

As you make decisions, your team wants to be in the loop and part of the process. Being transparent with what's happening will bring greater clarity to where you're headed. Explaining the "why" will further reveal your vulnerability and build confidence in you as a trusted leader, not a boss. Unsurprisingly, TMF has been named repeatedly on a variety of "best places to work" lists, such as the *Washingtonian* magazine and *Business Insider.*[263]

---

263 Alison Southwick, "Here's How the Motley Fool Landed on *INC.'s* Best Workplaces List," The Motley Fool, May 8, 2020.

LEAD BY EXAMPLE

"There is something only a CEO uniquely can do, which is set the tone, which can then capture the soul of the collective."

—SATYA NADELLA, CEO AT MICROSOFT

"To build a culture of trust, lead by example," Andrea Howe, founder of the Get Real Project, says. "You've got to be the trust that you want to see in the organization."[264] Also point out when others exemplify the kind of behavior you do and don't want to see.[265] You can't let poor behavior stand, but you also want to celebrate when someone does it right. This goes both ways. If your employee doesn't feel you're treating them well, they should be able to let you know.

Everyone you know has a story about not leading by example. Their manager (or parent) told them to do something and shortly after they discovered this was only a mandatory idea for one of you. Hypocrisy is not motivating. This will debilitate your current relationship and make building a future one difficult at best. As a manager, you need to make people aware when they do something wrong, but you have to live by the same rules.

---

264 Dori Meinert, "Why Trust Matters at Work: A Culture of Fear Hinders Innovation and Growth," Society for Human Resource Management, May 24, 2018.

265 Ibid.

Celebrate Awesome

"Catch somebody doing something right and then acknowledge it in front of everybody else," as Barron's Top Advisor Patti Brennan put it. If she finds someone going above and beyond, she brings everyone into their conference room to announce the extraordinary behavior that same day. She announces what the person did, how it connects to driving business, and presents them with a small yet coveted trophy along with a one-hundred-dollar bill.

Imagine being in that presentation and the impression this moment leaves on you, especially if you're a leader on her team. You'll not only seek this glory, but as a leader, you'll look for opportunities to celebrate your team members' contributions. This strategy doesn't just make people smile; it drives engagement. In the US, 37 percent of employees feel their manager focuses on their strengths, and 61 percent of that group feels engaged.[266] On average, 30 percent of US workers feel engaged in their jobs.[267] The upside potential is strong.

* * *

Enabling your team members is necessary to driving optimization, but they need to feel safe taking risks. Enablement is built on trusting you, feeling you know them, and that they have a voice. They need to know you approve of allocating time to finding a better way, and you need to lead by example.

---

266 Sorenson, "How Employees' Strengths."

267 Ibid.

This is all part of becoming a trusted advisor to your team. The goal is building a culture with a highly engaged team that seeks constant incremental change and one that isn't afraid to point out potential flaws in a plan. You'll know trust has evolved when others gain the confidence to bring creative ideas forward that challenge your thinking, with and without prompting. According to Paul Zak, the founding director of the Center for Neuroeconomics Studies, the benefits of trust at work include employees having 106 percent more energy and feeling 76 percent more engaged in their work.[268]

Once you've established trust and enabled optimization, it's on to empowering your team by letting them lead, promoting education, celebrating mistakes, and becoming a true trusted advisor to your team. These efforts will move your team up the learning curve consistently and collaboratively.

---

268 Paul J. Zak, "The Neuroscience of Trust," *Harvard Business Review*, January-February 2017.

CHAPTER 10

EMPOWER THE OPTIMIZER

———

"No person can be a great leader unless they take genuine joy in the successes of those under them."

—W. H. AUDEN

FREEDOM WITHIN A FRAMEWORK

After the Great Recession, competition was growing fierce from the low-cost exchange traded and index funds, and our asset management firm needed to evolve. My firm developed an industry-leading training strategy. The solution was to shift our sales approach to a consultative one to stay highly relevant to our clients. It was a huge commitment for everyone to change while simultaneously needing to deliver sales. Resistance was high as current efforts still appeared to be working. This was especially true with a remote workforce.

As each quarter passed, everyone on my team was challenged and given the freedom to find a way to effectively leverage this training as well as the new coaching workbooks and presentations provided to bring to our clients. We didn't know the right answer, but knew if we found a way, we could extract the intended value of this critical training initiative for the firm.

Recall the nine-dot exercise from earlier and the need to think differently. Two team members, Rick and Josh always took a creative approach to problem solving. Through repeated experiments, they found a stellar solution to embrace the new consulting model that would redefine their careers. They were not afraid to think "outside the box."

Here's the solution:[269]

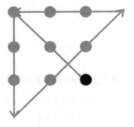

Instead of simply using the consulting training and tools in a traditional client meeting, they developed an entirely new model: an offsite training meeting. They literally took clients away from their offices for several hours to work "on

---

269 Sam Loyd, *Sam Loyd's Cyclopedia of 5000 Puzzles Tricks and Conundrums: With Answers* (New York: The Lamb Publishing Company, 1914), 380.

their business" rather than "in their business." Working in someone's office left the door open to too many distractions from phone calls, emails, and visitors. At the time, no other "salespeople" were conducting in-depth consulting meetings in our company or industry. Rick borrowed this idea from a top client, and he and Josh refined it until they made it highly impactful.

The offsite allowed for extreme focus on problem solving. Typical meetings were focused on educating clients on your products or financial market conditions. There was little industry focus on coaching the financial advisor on how to improve their team systems and processes.

This type of meeting required enormous work on the front end but completely changed their personal brands with the clients. This was a new inflection point and their business results entered another level of growth once these meetings became part of their sales process.

Let Them Lead
In an effort to drive greater adoption across our team, I asked both team members to present their "offsite" idea to their peers on a conference call. Interest was light during their presentation, as this required getting well outside one's comfort zone.

A few months later I asked them to do it again in a face-to-face meeting. They modified the presentation to better illustrate how the risk-reward relationship paid off. At that meeting, curiosity increased as Rick and Josh were delivering stellar sales results, and everyone knew it.

"How do you select the right client for an offsite meeting?" one team member asked.

"You need to pick a client that wants to grow and is willing to do the work," Rick replied. "You can't coach desire."

This dialogue eliminated a huge hurdle. *Who do I offer this complex solution to?*

Throughout the next quarter, I worked with each team member to identify three solid client targets. Uptake continued to be slow. It was frustrating, especially given the results that our two optimizers were finding. A major obstacle I found was people couldn't visualize leading this type of meeting. It was a massive change from the traditional product delivery meeting to which everyone was accustomed.

> *What problem are you facing that needs some out-of-the-box thinking?*

Own It

Driving down a small highway in central Pennsylvania on a business trip, I began to consider plans for my own upcoming team offsite meeting. I kept asking, "How can I use this meeting to meaningfully drive offsite adoption?" It struck me that we could have Rick and Josh run our internal offsite meeting for peers just as they would for their best clients. I immediately called them both to get their thoughts on the idea.

There was some early skepticism. Presenting in front of peers adds a new layer of pressure, but they rose to the occasion. Through several planning calls with our own sales consulting trainer, we put together our offsite road map. Both Rick and Josh conducted interviews with their peers in advance of the meeting, just as they would for their clients.

We needed to know the key issues to address during our training. We then built an agenda around those needs. The meeting was custom-made for the team. Everyone had a voice in the agenda and felt empowered.

Through the process of teaching their strategy to peers and leading the meeting, Rick and Josh elevated their own learning to better execute these meetings for clients in the future.

After this experiential learning, adoption of the new coaching concept finally ignited for our team, and others began to schedule their own offsite meetings.

An additional benefit was afforded to me as their leader and coach. This exercise revealed areas for specific training needs and was done in the spirit of learning together and building their meeting agenda, not me pointing out a weakness.

From the topics we covered during the training, I asked everyone to select the one item they wanted to work on with me during our recurring one-on-one coaching sessions.

Training someone on a self-selected topic gives them conviction. They own it and adoption comes much more easily.

From this day forward, training was customized to each person's self-selected needs, the offsite concept was adopted more broadly and optimizing together became a self-fulfilling prophecy.

The reason Rick and Josh found this remarkable solution was because they never stopped learning or experimenting in the spirit of improving how they deliver value for clients and drive business. They weren't afraid to think differently and help lift the (talent) curve for the team.

They were happy to share best practices with peers because that was the culture we developed. After our offsite, Josh quipped:

"We've developed a culture of innovation in how we are operating."

LEARNING AND GROWING

"Education is the most powerful weapon which you can use to change the world."

—NELSON MANDELA

Innovation is key to long-term success for any organization. Lifelong learning has the power to drive change and continuous improvement. To work, it must be embedded in your culture by developing trust within your team through open communication, building a process anchored in ongoing education and sustained through incorporating it into business planning.

Lifelong learning is not just occasional education, but consistent learning that will keep your team continuously reviewing your business with a fresh set of eyes and pushing forward. More importantly, you as a leader must be an example in learning and using that knowledge to take calculated risks.

How will you do this and know when this has taken hold in your company?

Let's explore.

Where Are We with Lifelong Learning?

According to a study by Pew Research Center, 74 percent of Americans consider themselves lifelong learners.[270] However, dig a little deeper and we find the majority of professional learners gain this title by simply taking on one new reading over a twelve-month period. Those that take a more formal approach largely do so to expand their network.[271]

An annual book can be additive and a larger network more powerful, for sure, but how much is this benefiting your

---

270 John B. Horrigan, "Lifelong Learning and Technology," *Pew Research Center,* March 22, 2016.

271 Ibid.

company versus your employee's next career move? The value in educating your team is that those insights not only expand networks and make team members more well-rounded, but also help lift the team. Rick and Josh never stopped learning, and through their success, they helped that mindset become contagious on our team.

How Has a Focus on Education Paid Off?

If you've ever wondered what a key driver to being one of the wealthiest countries in the world is, look no further than Singapore, a perennial world leader in education.[272] After decades under British rule, Singapore found itself with independent rule in 1959. After a failed attempt to become part of Malaysia, they were truly on their own in 1965.[273] Resources were limited, and they had few allies to ask for help. They had to survive with a culturally diverse population that was largely illiterate.[274]

Lee Kuan Yew, the country's first leader, set a plan that is still in force today. His goal: be highly relevant to the global economy. His core tactic: elevate the value of their one natural resource, their people. As senior economist Vishnu Varathan

272 "Singapore Overview," National Center on Education and the Economy, accessed May 28, 2020.

273 M.J., "How Singapore Gained Its Independence," *The Economist*, March 22, 2015.

274 "Singapore: Rapid Improvement Followed by Strong Performance," The Organization for Economic Co-operation and Development 2010, accessed May 23, 2020.

described Yew's work, "His defining economic policy is arguably the uncompromising standards for universally accessible, top-flight public education systems."[275]

Singapore's land mass is smaller than the five boroughs of New York City.[276] They've been bound by constraints, yet they've not only survived, they thrived—through education. They have one of the most educated and wealthiest populations on the planet, and they started in extreme poverty just a few decades ago.

In short, there is a high correlation between countries leading in education and high incomes.[277] This is a powerful model. It can be adopted elsewhere, but it has to be done in a style that works for you, your team, and your budget.

As Singapore has displayed, education is key to innovation and prosperity. However, a central part of their strategy includes engaging their populace in the process. They set a plan, execute it, and solicit feedback periodically to increase their chances of success and develop buy-in with the new practices.[278] If their plan isn't working, they are not afraid to

275 Zarina Hussain, "How Lee Kuan Yew Engineered Singapore's Economic Miracle," *BBC News*, March 24, 2015.

276 *Nations Encyclopedia Online, s.v.* "Singapore," accessed September 15, 2020.

277 United Nations Development Programme, "Human Development Reports," Human Development Index Trends, 1990-2018, table 2, accessed May 27, 2020.

278 Regina Tan, "iGov: The Singapore Model for Online Intersection Between Government and Public," Columbia University New Media and Development Communication, accessed May 29, 2020.

reevaluate and change course. Singapore never stops trying to improve on every of aspect of their economy.

As part of my MBA program, the final project my team chose was researching how Singapore was using big data to run their Smart City initiative. A team of seven spent months conducting research and phone interviews and then spent a week doing live interviews in Singapore.

A pivot we found firsthand was with the Smart City office. The day before our meeting with them, they called me to reschedule. The Singapore government wasn't seeing the pace of progress they wanted from the group and restructured the reporting lines to make the team more "integrated and responsive." This was less than six months after a prior restructuring.

> *Singapore doesn't wait for others to disrupt them, they do it themselves. They educate their people, empower innovation, cause self-disruption, and repeat again and again.*

How Do We Embed Lifelong Learning into Our Company?
If education is the key to innovation and ultimately success, how do you embed this mindset in your team? Ask them! The answers here will be enriched when asked after building trust.

- What learning topics or designations are most relevant to your career?
- How do you learn most effectively? Formal versus informal?
- What learning have you done on your own? Why?

Once you've gathered this insight, you need to build a coalition to develop your learning roadmap. Start with your people that already embrace learning, they're likely your top performers. They will help this idea gain credibility. Schedule two or three meetings to capture their insights and develop your plan.

As this group generates ideas for the learning journey, schedule time to have the coalition introduce the continuing education ideas and lead discussions with the rest of the team. Have them share their own educational experience and solicit new ideas. Yes, as the team leader, take a back seat here. This will further develop those top performers and remove the obstacle of this new learning initiative being "from their boss."

Budget constraints are a given, so you need to be creative. Invite the coalition to think outside the box and have a voice in the discussion. Ideas can range from study groups and book clubs to designations and formal degrees. Be curious and find what works for the team by asking.

If you have the budget, be sure to use the $5,250 tangible tax benefits to educating your team.[279] Your company can deduct the expense and the benefit is not taxable to the employee.[280] Offer this money as an incentive for team members to receive educational funding if they hit certain targets you set.

---

279 Troy Onink, "Get $5,250 A Year from Your Employer to Pay for College," *Forbes*, June 30, 2015.

280 Ibid.

There will be bumps as learning develops and new methods are attempted, but as your team continues this journey and you foster a collaborative effort built on trust, learning will grow more efficiently and the output more effective.

According to Jesse Nieminen, co-founder and Chairman of Viima, an innovation management software company, to increase the ongoing value of learning, chart the factors affecting performance of a role. Use that information as a basis for letting team members evaluate their progress and results and then self-select areas of improvement.

Additionally, have your coalition provide input into what will be measured and have each team member share what they are working on in the upcoming period. These steps will help them take ownership of their learning, align it with education that has proven effective in driving business results, and inspire others to join the journey by showing we all have room for improvement.

You'll know this has taken root when your less innovative team members begin to come to you with new ideas. They trust you enough to try and fail, and they've embraced education enough to open their minds to exploring new possibilities.

Many of your team members will surprise not just you and the team, but themselves. This surprise will occur as they discover better ideas and methods never thought possible, as we saw with the offsite training concept. As an added benefit, those who don't engage in the learning journey will help you as the leader see more clearly how well they fit your plan for growth and their potential to add to the team going forward.

Everyone who took my challenge to earn an advanced designation had some reservations at the start. Each person came back and thanked me for helping them embrace the learning journey and several went on to add further designations.

THE TRUSTED ADVISOR

Define, Don't Solve
There is a bright orange sticky note sitting on my screen right now that lists three open-ended questions: what, why, and how. A few examples:

- What exactly is it you're trying to solve?
- Why is this issue so important?
- How have you tried to solve this so far?

Having worked with a remote team for years, most conversations have been on video chats or calls. In a world that only gets busier, you often feel you're operating with very limited time, so when your team members call you with issues, you must fight the urge to provide solutions and instead coach them to find their own way.

One team member I inherited in a reorganization, we'll call him Bob, would not only get defensive when I'd ask these questions, on one occasion he threw it back me. He had an unhappy top client, and we set time to discuss progress.

"Bob, how is resolution coming with Jeff's issue?"

"It's going ok."

"Is it fixed?"

"Not yet."

"What do you think would move it along?"

"What do YOU think would move it along?" he shot back.

There was trust-building yet to be done with Bob.

That bright sticky note sits on my screen as a constant reminder to practice this effort and keep me centered in heated moments. Asking additional open-ended questions helps get closer to the root of the issue and provides greater context for both parties. It's quite possible a few simple questions could lead them to a solution without your actual input.

"This is a tricky one. How frustrated do you think your client is with this issue?" I asked.

"Very."

"How do you think he would handle this if he was dealing with a similar issue for one of his top clients?"

"He'd create a plan with his service team with deadlines and daily check-ins for progress."

"How might that strategy help you here?"

Silence.

"I've got a plan to build!"

With a road map, it took Bob another week of daily commitment to resolve the issue. The client was satisfied and stayed on board. Losing that client would have devastated his sales results that year.

Help your team see the real issue they are facing and why. In Bob's case, he was not taking ownership. Use open ended questions to guide them to the answer.

> *If you simply give them a solution, you're teaching them to bring their problems to you. It may make you feel important, but it is inefficient.*

This strategy works best with a foundation of trust with your team members. Without trust, asking open-ended questions can create negative energy and defensive posture, as I found with Bob.

With trust, you will begin to see the proverbial light bulb going off above their heads as you ask questions to get them to think more openly about their problem.

A leader's job isn't solving every issue for their team but being a trusted advisor and developing thoughtful leaders. A trusted advisor's role is to work on "problem definition, not problem solution."[281] Much like the feedback conversations, this gets easier over time.

Set Boundaries

Philip Holt from Microsoft commits the time and resources to understanding his team, their strengths, and the scope of each project. He then builds impactful structures to make the work happen and to get everyone to constantly optimize decisions to improve their game. All the while, making his team feel highly engaged in the execution and empowered to challenge ideas he brings forth and entirely within boundaries that all can see clearly. Mr. Holt believes:

"The more boundaries you can place around a problem, the more it frees you to find new and innovative solutions. If you hand someone a blank sheet of paper and say draw a picture, the response is likely, I don't know what to draw. If you say, draw a tree, now they can get a lot more creative about making a tree."

Total freedom is a difficult place to begin and has a high probability of creating work that doesn't deliver the desired value. You need to establish boundaries with guidance. Mr. Holt went on to conclude, "So the more constraints and boundaries that you apply to the creative space, I think the more empowering it is actually. Which is ironic."

---

281 Pete Marcus, "Eight Steps to Becoming a Trusted Advisor," (blog) Harvard - tech communications agency, September 25, 2017.

Celebrate Mistakes

Katrina has spent her entire professional career working to improve public education with a passion to make the experience more impactful for children and teachers. She has never stopped trying to better herself and has found the simple act of constantly learning to generate many fantastic ideas over the years. Every idea hasn't been a smashing success, but she sees it as a learning experience.

She is now a principal and has empowered her team with this philosophy. "We need to continue to grow so we can better help our students." She's made it clear that with new ideas comes failure, and she has worked with her team to "celebrate mistakes," focus on what they learned and refine what they've done. Every staff meeting is dedicated to a safe discussion on new efforts, what has worked, what has not, and what has been learned.

Her staff is about forty-five people, and like any organization, she has people across the bell curve with varying degrees of interest in innovating and driving change. She has a few informal leaders who help her keep a pulse on current issues and work with her to come up with collaborative strategies to drive solutions. One particular leader is Susan. She is a specialty teacher that moves from class to class, so she has a unique perspective of the school.

This past school year there was an uptick in negative behavior, and Katrina was trying to understand why. She began to look at how issues were addressed and set up an exercise to capture these insights from her entire team. She was careful not to single people out or get caught in negative storytelling.

So, in a staff meeting, she created groups of people to get all their ideas on butcher paper. After the session, she gathered the insights and summarized them into key themes.

She wanted to learn what the staff was really trying to say, what they were looking to learn more about, and what actions they felt would be effective in improving the behavior situation. A common theme for action was to make better connections with the children and families. She found a book called *Creating the School Family* by Dr. Becky Bailey and gave each staff-member a copy. Katrina hadn't developed a game plan yet with the book but felt it was worth everyone reading.

In the midst of the global pandemic, Susan came to her one day and asked, "Can we do a study group on the book you shared? I can set it up." Katrina said, "Let's try it." Katrina had spent the last eight years building a trusting relationship with Susan, and Susan is a "real go-getter." This was a great relationship, where innovation could blossom.

Susan offered three options to attend a two-part book session. The idea was to create smaller, more intimate groups. The first session had mixed levels of engagement, so she met with Katrina to brainstorm how to improve on round two. They decided to give team members more specific content to study and share with everyone. This not only drove engagement, but also opened the door to finding a solution to enhancing the rules.

They found through this exercise that the current stated rules were too abstract for the students: be safe, be respectful, be responsible. Behind these three big ideas were 157 rules that no one could memorize. Through the book club and several iterations of ideas, they found much more actionable words for the students to live by: make positive connections, problem-solving with others, and being safe.

As they roll out these new standards, there's no doubt Katrina and her team will observe and measure the results to look for improvement, "celebrate mistakes," and make changes, if necessary.

* * *

Empowering your team is not easy, and without trust, it's bordering impossible. Leaders need to be brave enough to let others lead, aware enough to know that learning never ends, and patient enough to know that developing into a trusted advisor is more powerful than directing traffic.

You cannot overlook that with innovation comes failure. When that moment arrives, don't chastise your team for failing; celebrate them for trying something new. Like Thomas Edison, they now know a way that doesn't work. Showcase curiosity so new knowledge is found and shared. These strategies create the safe environment needed to empower your team to find stronger solutions, take calculated risks, and help navigate the company through inevitable challenges.

As your team grows more engaged and empowered, you need to keep momentum. In chapter eleven, we will explore how to sustain the optimizer mindset in your team and embed it in your culture.

CHAPTER 11

SUSTAINING A CULTURE OF OPTIMIZATION

———

PROCESS, PROCESS, PROCESS

What's your favorite restaurant? How often do you go there versus other options? Why? I can't tell you how often my family and I ate at the same Italian restaurant near our old house. We felt like its kitchen was an extension of our home. The space was warm and welcoming, and the service casual yet excellent. The menu is inventive and inviting. Meal selection was always a delightful challenge, and the staff happily helped us navigate the options to find just the right choice.

How do they deliver every time? They have recipes and processes they've established and refined. Even with employee turnover, the systems stay the same and new hires are taught. The steps are clearly laid out on how to execute, and the staff is trained extensively on how to provide a memorable experience. Making a meal or serving a table often go unnoticed and appear simple unless something doesn't meet your expectations. Then you learn the true value of the training and processes the restaurant has in place.

As a restaurant owner or business leader, you must create processes to sustain how you lead and develop optimization. This is how you move your business forward year after year and embed this mindset in your team. In this effort, carve out time to harness creativity and drive outside-the-box thinking across your team. This generates new ideas and pulls your team deeper into the mission.

WHY IS THERE SUCH AN ISSUE WITH A PROCESS?

"Fix the process, not the problem."
—HAROLD SIRKIN & GEORGE STALK, JR.[282]

If you aren't getting the desired results from your team, there is likely a process and progress challenge somewhere. Your team is unclear on exactly how to execute the mission, what roles and responsibilities each person has, and training is likely insufficient. Or worse yet, your team doesn't observe process thinking in your culture or doesn't see the value in it for them. Few things could drive inefficiency more. This can be overcome, but it won't be done quickly.

---

282 Harold L. Sirkin and George Stalk Jr., "Fix the Process, Not the Problem," *Harvard Business Review*, July-August 1990.

A business leader may appear successful, but it's possible that, due to lack of structure, the team lives in a constant emergency-room mode that is hidden from outsiders. Burnout is hiding in plain sight. In a recent survey of 7,500 full-time employees, 23 percent feel burnt out "often or always," and 44 percent say "sometimes."[283] This is not sustainable.

The Duck

Carolyn, a veteran financial services professional, made a career change recently and joined a large financial advisory practice. With their meticulously designed lobby and large number of well-dressed team members, this team gives a solid first impression. Carolyn was brought in to help develop greater processes and structure to help the team execute more effectively and increase growth. During the interview, the team presented nearly flawlessly, and she wondered what could possibly need fixing.

Soon after joining and seeing behind the curtain, she realized there were issues around almost every corner. Systems to onboard clients and manage client relationships were vague. The lead advisor was very charismatic and had a gift for networking and attracting new clients but didn't excel at managing operations. Once the clients' money arrived, it was a fire drill managing each step in the background to make the client feel like they had a premium experience.

---

283 Ben Wigert and Sangeeta Agrawal, "Employee Burnout, Part 1: The 5 Main Causes," *Gallup*, July 12, 2018.

The team was constantly working overtime to keep clients satisfied, but they were treading water at best. This is known as the "Duck Syndrome;" on the surface, the duck appears graceful and calm but under the water they are kicking furiously.[284] This team leader made Carolyn realize, "In order to get better, you have to admit there are things you don't do well."

The leader wasn't opposed to investing in his business to improve operations. Each time he attended an educational conference, the team waited in fear, wondering what new tool or idea would be thrown at them to "fix the problems." The new tools and ideas had good intentions, but you must have the structure, buy-in, and leadership in place to effectively manage and communicate change. Simply adding a new tool and hoping for the best won't do it.

Carolyn spent weeks identifying bottlenecks, communication missteps, and the gaps in systems for running the business. She brought her insights to the principal's attention on several occasions, yet he continuously postponed the meeting because he "had no time." She couldn't even begin a discussion on how to fix the systemic failures she was hired to address.

The work piled up as new clients came in and the daily fire drills continued with no end in sight. Realizing this owner wasn't committed to the required cultural mindset shift,

---

284 Caroline Beaton, "Millennial Duck Syndrome," *Psychology Today*, May 20, 2017.

Carolyn left after a few months for a fantastic opportunity. Within weeks at her new role, she began implementing new operational procedures to streamline her new processes.

When systems aren't established and no one takes ownership, resentment sets in and finger-pointing begins. In reality, it's not flawed people, it's a flawed process they don't understand. Let's look at what a constant focus on process improvement looks like.

WHAT ARE THE BENEFITS OF A WELL-DEFINED PROCESS?

Amancio Ortega is the son of a railroad worker and a maid with no formal higher education. Today, he is the sixth wealthiest person in the world, with a net worth over seventy billion dollars.[285] Mr. Ortega doesn't compete with Warren Buffet in business, create software, or own a social media company. He owns about 60 percent of Zara, the largest fashion retailer on the planet, and avoids the spotlight.[286]

He began his career delivering and manufacturing textiles through a small family business in 1963, in a quiet northwest corner of Spain, and he started Zara in 1975.[287] Early

---

285 "The World's Real-Time Billionaire," *Forbes*, accessed September 18, 2020.

286 Katie Warren and Melissa Wiley, "Meet Amancio Ortega, the Fiercely Private Zara Founder Who's Worth $68.5 Billion and Owns Properties in Madrid, London, and New York City," *Business Insider*, October 29, 2019.

287 Suzy Hansen, "How Zara Grew Into the World's Largest Fashion Retailer," *The New York Times*, November 9, 2012, sec. Magazine.

on, he observed the various stages of the textile business and learned value in controlling each step of making clothing.[288] Controlling more of the supply chain allows for greater cost management and speed of delivery.

In the early 1960s, Ortega became the manager of a luxury clothing store that few could afford.[289] He recognized a broader market for these clothing styles. Soon, he began to make similar products with lower-cost goods.[290] Affordability in fashion was a problem for most people, and Ortega solved it.

Zara's strategy for success is clear, as CEO Pablo Isla shared, "Find out what our customers want, and design, produce, and distribute it quickly."[291] This works when roles and responsibilities are well-articulated, the mission is understood by all, and leaders are not afraid of letting their team members lead.

According to Mr. Isla, the management system is simple: "We empower our people at all levels to make thousands of decisions every day."[292] This culture requires vulnerable leaders who are willing to give up control and grant decision-ownership to their teams to flourish.

---

288 "Amancio Ortega 1936— Biography - Early Career, The Zara Phenomenon, Inditex," accessed September 18, 2020.

289 Ibid.

290 Ibid.

291 Kasra Ferdows, Jose A.D. Machuca, and Michael A. Lewis, "ZARA: The World's Largest Fashion Retailer," 2014.

292 Ibid.

They are not afraid to hire young people and give them lots of responsibility. The finance director, Miguel Diaz, explains, "You don't have to be a star to work here, but you must be competent and have an entrepreneurial spirit."[293] In fact, 60 percent of the workforce is thirty or younger.[294]

They don't hire based on age and experience to run this empire; they bring in motivated people who want to build something excellent. This is in stark contrast to competitors like H&M and Gap that have a chief designer from whom new ideas flow.[295] With a sole decision maker, team members are not empowered and must wait to take action.

Zara has developed a super-agile supply chain that requires innovation end-to-end and distributed decision making.[296] The decisions must be shared for speed. Zara can put the latest fashion in customers' hands within four to six weeks.[297] Most competitors take months to do the same. This speed takes constant focus on optimization, and to deliver, you need guardrails that the systems furnish. These systems provide clarity of the mission and drive efficiency, effectiveness, and engagement for 176,000 employees.[298]

---

293 Ibid.

294 Pamela N. Danziger, "Why Zara Succeeds: It Focuses On Pulling People In, Not Pushing Product Out," *Forbes*, accessed September 18, 2020.

295 Hau L. Lee, "How Extreme Agility Put Zara Ahead in Fast Fashion," December 10, 2019.

296 Ibid.

297 Ibid.

298 "Our Employees - Inditex.Com," accessed September 18, 2020.

Similar to The Motley Fool, Zara believes they can always improve. They saw the benefit in continuous interactions with designers, buyers (sourcing and production), and country managers, and they reorganized their headquarters to physically put each of these groups in the same room, encouraging impromptu meetings.[299] This allows designers to create new ideas, buyers to quickly approve or disapprove them, and country managers to ship them to the right stores. They know where to ship because they're in constant contact with store managers.[300]

This system is predicated on paying close attention to customers and their needs. They have evolved from a product focus to the four Es: Experience, Exchange, Evangelism, and Every Place.[301] This strategy puts the customer at the center of every decision. They've created a variety of digital interactions in-store with augmented-reality-enabled shop windows and an app to virtually try-on clothing. "Zara excels by pulling customers into the brand, rather than pushing products."[302]

Pull all this optimization of processes together, and what do you have? A company that operates so efficiently that they generate "negative operating working capital."[303] Zara col-

---

299 Ferdows, Machuca, and Lewis, "ZARA: The World's Largest Fashion Retailer."

300 Ibid.

301 Danziger, "Why Zara Succeeds."

302 Ibid.

303 Ferdows, Machuca, and Lewis, "ZARA: The World's Largest Fashion Retailer."

lects cash faster than they have to pay it out, which is highly unusual in any industry, much less the fashion industry. They have over seven thousand stores worldwide.[304] Those stores have shoppers visit two- to three-times more often than top competitors, and they've amassed over forty million followers on Instagram, a leading social media platform.[305]

This is all made possible by building a strong leadership culture—one that is not afraid to fail and that learns along every step of the journey. The leadership team exhibits constant vulnerability, as evidenced by Mr. Isla. "We are far from perfect. Whatever we analyze, we see lots of room for improvement. Continuous improvement is in the heart of the company."[306] Leadership styles are contagious, good or bad. This is a culture of serial optimizers that leads to sustain excellence.

HOW TO USE A PROCESS TO DRIVE OPTIMIZATION?

How do you develop a consistent approach to creating a culture of optimizers? Put it in writing.

Each year, when business-plan-writing time arrived, I made a special request to my team to add a section outside of the traditional planning template. The request was to include

---

304 "Inditex around the World - Inditex.Com," accessed September 18, 2020

305 Danziger, "Why Zara Succeeds."

306 Ferdows, Machuca, and Lewis, "ZARA: The World's Largest Fashion Retailer."

one or two specific opportunities to help them operate more efficiently and effectively in the coming year.

One opportunity can be a personal goal: "How are you going to evolve this year?" After fleshing this idea out with a peer, Mike, he added a solid twist: "With this innovation, what will you stop doing?" This creates much finer thinking around optimizing. If I am adding work to my plate, what is the full cost and benefit?

When this add-on was new, many business plans were returned for further review. One team member, Chris, submitted that he wanted to "get in better shape this year." It provided a coaching opportunity to talk through planning.

What are your specific goals? How will you measure success? How often will you measure? How many days each week will you exercise? How well does your diet align with your goals? Will you work out at home or hire a trainer?

Through these questions about his personal goal, he learned how to better plan for his business goal. That year, he achieved a key multi-million-dollar initiative in sales for the first time and got a smaller belt.

Expressing learning as part of this journey is critical. Set the tone that:

> *Evolving our skills does not occur in a straight line, and that's okay. We will learn from our challenges and grow as a team.*

Your business plan as a leader also requires two additional sections. One, how will you, the leader, evolve this year? Two, how will you, the leader, hold your team and yourself accountable? After the goals are established in writing, use biweekly one-on-one calls to check-in on individuals and measure their progress against goals, including specific optimization goals.

These calls are also an opportunity for you as a leader to have your team help hold you accountable for the new initiatives you've established for yourself. This exercise will further demonstrate your vulnerability and empower your team to have a voice in your business, propelling your growth as a trusted advisor. The final critical element to these calls is to do them with a goal of progress, not judgement.

As the new ideas evolve in the coming weeks, make time to let them share the journey, including the struggles. This will deepen the value of this planning concept to the team, help them see they are not alone, and build mutual respect. Watching a team member overcome a struggle in front of you is a powerful tool for solidarity.

This sharing will help the team better understand the learning they've done, encourage the rest to continue or join in this experience, and help others understand the value of serial optimization.

Opportunity Requires Flexibility

Change demands resources. You need to allocate part of your budget as flexible to make this work, and your team needs to know this. Each year, I held back part of the team's budget to allow for intra-year reallocation of money without asking anyone to give something up. Additionally, at the midpoint of the year and after the third quarter, I asked for specific estimates to find if they would have money left over at the year's end, or if they had a great opportunity requiring further resources.

These budget chats gave me a solid glimpse into how far ahead and how strategic each team member was in business planning, and it gave them a sense of urgency. If you could make a solid case for a larger budget, we could make it work. In the first half of the year, I had the money set aside already. In the second half, it was coming out of someone else's budget. This strategy provides exceptional latitude to be opportunistic with innovative ideas throughout the year. Transparency makes these shifts easier.

As Dean Paul Almeida of the Georgetown Business School and strategy professor shared, "You can't be afraid to change course as you never know what challenge or opportunity may appear," and "You have to be flexible with your budget to allow for pivots throughout the year." This isn't easy.

Innovation drives success and implementing a process to enable, empower, and sustain it is critical to the journey. You'll know this concept has taken hold when sharing amongst your team grows without a push from you. They'll pull each other.

BUILDING TEAMWORK

Developing your team to shift their mindset takes everyone working together, not just a select few. We've seen how powerful trust is for a leader working with their team; it's equally relevant to build within your team. Strategies to help build a team that grows together include a mentoring program, study groups, and walking in others' shoes.

Mentor

Kyle, a former NCAA football player, was an early mentee of mine. He was hungry and ready to learn and, unsurprisingly, a bit raw. We established expectations at our first meeting along with his goals. He came to each meeting well-prepared with several strategic and tactical questions for me. What? Why? How? I would ask him to problem-define and not problem-solve. It was solid practice for me to not only hone my trusted advisor skills, but to explore creative ways to challenge others on my team.

He was feeling stalled on his next promotion, and we collaboratively unearthed training opportunities for him. We set a challenge for him to use a subsection of the new training I was working on with my team. In this case, we agreed on trying relationship-development questions with at least three clients until we spoke again.

During our next call, I could feel his enthusiasm pouring through the phone as he told me, "I engaged one of our top clients with these questions. We've never spoken so long." He continued to embrace every challenge I put in front of him and always asked me thoughtful questions about career and business decisions I had made. Kyle was promoted within a year of our engagement.

Study Groups

Study groups amongst your team can provide growth for many and a safe outlet for discussing challenges. This idea came from surveying my team about improving our recurring conference calls. This is a call with all your team members, but no managers attend. It's a chance for your team to informally brainstorm together on challenges with their peers without the pressure of having their boss observing. Assign one team member to lead, or emcee, the call. Consider choosing someone who has leadership aspirations to run at least one call but give everyone an opportunity over time.

This will push them out of their comfort zone and get them to think more creatively about how to best manage the call and understand the pressure you feel to lead calls. After the pilot call, I asked for feedback on how it went. The consensus was to have two study group calls each year, and we did.

Warning: don't follow up with team members to inquire about any negative topics that came up on the study group call beyond what needs fixing to help future calls be more impactful.

Walk in Their Shoes

Spending time in another's shoes is eye opening. A top team member came to me one day and asked if he could travel with a peer to learn. The cynic in me wondered if this was a mini vacation, but once we explored the thoughtful game plan, it made perfect sense. He clearly explained that his peer had been very successful building business with a client firm he found challenging, and he needed a fresh approach.

They developed a targeted list of sales calls for their time together, and he got on a plane. The trip was done in one overnight stay, and the learning was exceptional. Upon his return, he felt refreshed with a new approach and immediately went to work refining his business objectives, and he quickly yielded results. This exercise got me to think further about the unique skills of each team member and how their skills could complement each other.

I offered for other team members to try out the new idea and team-up with a peer. Several team members scheduled joint travel days or reached out to peers that appeared to have complementary skills to their own. This won't assure overnight success, but it will promote the growth of teamwork amongst your team. This exercise acts as a reminder that you can learn from anyone on the team through curiosity and vulnerability.

WORK ON PURPOSE

José Pires was born in Rio de Janeiro, Brazil, and is the father of five children. He was educated in the US and has spent most of his life there. He is a former Fortune 100 executive who developed and implemented global, award-winning innovation programs. As the founder and CEO of Global Excellence & Innovation, he has worked with hundreds of cross-industry organizations in more than twenty countries and developed over thirty thousand excellence and innovation leaders in the last two decades.

After helping build cultures of excellence and innovation in business, non-profits, and governments globally, he fully appreciates the formidable challenges of mastering the complexities of innovation acceleration: "There is no silver bullet to innovation. 90 percent of innovation is execution."

According to Pires, there are three levels of innovation in an organization: one, have the star innovator or entrepreneur that makes it happen; two, build systems to scale the ideas; and three, develop a culture of excellence and innovation.

To build this culture, Jose works closely with senior leaders in the organizations to create an environment of inclusion, diversity, and collaboration, with a clear meritocracy of ideas and disciplined execution mechanisms, accessible to all. If your idea is approved, you can allocate 20 percent of time to this project.

The employee must strategically align, nurture, and develop their idea to move forward, "similar to the show *Shark Tank*, but with less drama." They intentionally make the process difficult, as they want to increase the chance of a project being seen all the way through. José counseled,

"Successful innovation leaders are only revealed by the test of execution. They have purpose, passion, discipline, and resilience."

You need to inspire and welcome innovation, build systems to manage the ideas, and people to steward them to completion. He shared,

> "*A real success is when you can align a person's purpose with that of the company.*"

While accelerating innovation in a multi-billion-dollar transformation with an energy company, José met an accountant from corporate finance. We'll call him Jeff. As part of José's work, he asked Jeff, "What do you look forward to doing every day?" Jeff replied, "I can't wait to get home and work on one of my boat engines." Jeff loves refurbishing boat engines, one after another, even though it makes no economic sense.

José was curious and asked Jeff, "Are you aware of the marine operations in our company?" Jeff said, "Yes," but he's "not connected to the marine group and would love to learn more." José guided him to "explore the marine group, and if you discover an opportunity to create value that aligns with your purpose, we'll look at it."

Jeff explored several ideas and found significant potential value in an "under-keel" clearance project for oil tankers. Large ships need to have specific, minimum clearances from the bottom of the ocean for safety measures while navigating ports. This distance changes with displacement as you load the ship.

Within months, Jeff collaboratively led a small team to develop a new technology that better scanned the ocean floor, allowing for additional clearance. Ships could carry significantly more oil and still safely get in and out the ports. When Jeff set to work on this project, he spent the 20 percent time he was allocated, plus his nights and weekends. He toiled through a series of iterations and explored a variety of ideas until he found a significant win because he loved the work.

The extra oil these ships now hauled created tens of millions in additional earnings for the organization each year. Connecting the dots for this level of success was complex, took enormous creativity, high levels of collaborative leadership within and outside the organization, and had a high level of success due to a disciplined process for innovation.

* * *

"Nothing in the world is worth having or worth doing unless it means effort, pain, and difficulty."
                                                    —THEODORE ROOSEVELT

Driving innovation is complex. Establishing processes, systems, roles, and responsibilities to deliver takes time and buy-in from everyone. Your team needs to learn to work together and be inspired to pull each other along, and as a leader, you can facilitate that. No setup is perfect, and patience will be a hurdle in this day and age of short-term goals.

Building a process to systematically drive innovation can unleash the potential in your team, build collaboration, and perpetuate durable results. Combining a process for enabling innovation, discovering a purpose for your company, and helping employees align their purpose to it is how you sustain a culture of optimization.

CONCLUSION

———

"Leadership is a series of behaviors rather than a role for heroes."
—MARGARET WHEATLEY

Steve had been with the firm several years and was an industry veteran. I inherited him in an internal reorganization. It did not take long to discover his unique abilities to gain a deep technical understanding of our products, develop rich context around the story with outside learning, and make an incredibly compelling argument for why a client should make a purchase. He was always happy to share his ideas with peers, and he took the time to earn several professional designations.

When the industry took a dramatic turn to low-cost products after the Great Recession in 2008, the firm created a new path forward to fight for relevance. We adopted the consulting-versus-sales model. Steve was slow to embrace this evolution. His previous efforts had created success for many years. However, being a product expert in the current climate lost tremendous value versus five to ten years ago. Information is too easy to find, and client needs have become more complex. The necessary value proposition for our firm had evolved into coaching clients on making their own business run much more efficiently and effectively.

Steve and I had many coaching conversations about professional growth. Progress was slow at first. The turning point for him came with an opportunity to lead. After asking the team how to improve our conference call schedule, I also asked how to make the calls more engaging. A great idea came forward to let each team member lead a monthly call throughout the year.

The rotating call leader chose the topic and led the entire session, other than brief introductory comments by me. The team members usually called me to fine-tune their idea before the group call, but I purposely didn't require it. I wanted them to take ownership and see how they embraced the opportunity. These preparation calls often provided tactical coaching moments to ask further open-ended questions, encourage broader thinking, and get them to seek peer feedback on what to present.

As each team member put their agenda together and presented it to their peers, others took note of the value of their ideas. They knew they were going to be in the same position soon and wanted to bring even more value to the calls. No one wanted to lead the call that everyone said wasn't useful. This drove creativity and helped the team grow.

Steve's turn was coming up, and he did not reach out to me to fine-tune his idea. I was a bit nervous about how he was going to deliver. He had reached out to his peers and found no one used a particular efficiency-driving technology we had access to; many didn't even know we had access to it. He took the time to incorporate the tool in his own business and brought in an expert from our technology training group to co-present the idea. Leveraging his story-telling strength, Steve made a very compelling case as to why we should use this new tool, and all but two team members ended up adopting it.

Steve didn't bring the greatest idea the team had ever seen. What he did do, through our process of building trust and challenging each other to constantly improve, was find an opportunity for everyone to elevate their productivity. He made them aware of an efficiency-driving tool and how and why we should put it to use immediately.

* * *

Not everyone on your team will bring the most innovative idea forward. That's okay. The real goal is getting them to continuously think creatively and collaboratively. Each person is not built to go on this journey. Some will embrace this culture and others will choose to find a new career opportunity for themselves that better aligns with their passion and natural value proposition.

However, if you can create a safe environment and a culture of serial optimizers, they have a strong chance of working and developing together, as Steve displayed. This process isn't limited to those on your team that need to grow the most; it can help everyone elevate their skills as we saw with top performers Rick and Josh.

Building and leading a team of serial optimizers to execute innovation can be a powerful force for any organization. Focusing on incremental steps can help overcome the emotional toll of change. With this mindset, it is easier to embrace and grow adoption when the inevitable larger initiatives come along.

Serial optimization is so critical because of these reasons. As you plan, you need to be aware of emotional barriers, and break them down by focusing on building trust between each team member and their peers as well as building trust between yourself and the team.

We saw emotional reaction play out in how the "devil's drink," or coffee, was demonized upon arrival to Europe, as it disrupted incumbent products and social order. What it really came down to was people feeling a loss of the comfort of what they knew and how much control they had over their population. Control and trust are fragile elements and developing and maintaining them within your organization is a never-ending journey.

The good news is people can be adaptable with the proper motivation, vision, and guidance. You must help your team clearly see that the benefits of transforming outweigh the costs of the additional effort. Giving them a voice in the journey is key. When given a voice, ownership of the idea grows, and with that, adoption can accelerate.

We learned the key principles of the serial optimizer. The optimizer is vulnerable, looks to solve real problems, is customer-centric in all work, and has an extreme focus on excellence. These are the skills that need to be sought after, developed, and grown within your team. Embedding your team with these skills will create a positive cycle that will take on momentum of its own. Once this energy takes off, your role will shift more to managing boundaries, as opposed to managing optimization.

To foster the growth of these skills in your team, you need to establish systems to execute and a high level of camaraderie. To increase your chances of finding success year after year with innovation, you must build optimization into your business plan for sustainability. Part of each year's planning needs to include how your team will evolve and better work together.

Building a culture of optimization allows you to harness your teams' creativity. To maximize this effort, your budget needs flexibility to allow for pivots and to be reallocated throughout the year to capitalize on innovation. A process is needed to surface, test, adopt, and support the new ideas. Collaboration is a must to effectively instill new strategies into your current operations and to grow adoption across your team.

Disrupting one's self with new ideas does not come naturally to everyone. Singapore, a world leader in self disruption, has not had an easy journey. Therefore, you need to embed this mindset of perpetual improvement into your team, always with a focus on making your employees and customers feel like part of the journey. The trust you build with each team member and your relationship with them fosters an environment in which they feel safe. As you become a trusted advisor to your team, you empower a new set of leaders who embrace lifelong learning, and you sustain success by building serial optimization into the yearly planning process and culture.

* * *

Creating a culture of optimizers won't solve all of your problems, but if you can incorporate these strategies, you'll find a team that operates with a growth mindset, consistently working to upskill themselves and their business. This team will challenge each other to push the envelope to get better, and they will want to help each other. This process needs guidance but has the ability to take on a life of its own, pull your team along, and deliver impactful results with broad support as it evolves.

Change will always get you out of your comfort zone, and you might find yourself standing in a dark room hosting a party for one thousand people outside of your industry. This can be an unsettling experience, but if you stay focused on learning and growing and embrace the moment, you might find yourself with a new way to think outside the box, lifting the curve for yourself and your team.

ACKNOWLEDGEMENTS

———

This book represents optimization in its very creation, and I have many to thank for that. The dozens of people who took the time to be interviewed and brainstorm with me provided enormous value to my thinking on the book as well as rich stories. Thanks to all of you.

A few folks deserve a special mention. The book's origins come from Kamal Bhatia's first suggesting I write a leadership paper. I wrote the paper and shared it with a long-time friend, Michael Gottesman, who suggested it could be a series. I wrote the series and took it to another friend with expertise in publishing papers, Nick Yaeger. We spent hours refining the series.

From there, I shared the series with Professor Prashant Malayvia who suggested I had the makings of a book. He introduced me to Eric Koester, founder of the Creator Institute, and I couldn't help but be drawn to Eric's energy and enthusiasm for creating. Thanks to each of them for encouraging me to push further and get outside of my comfort zone.

The relentless work of my beta reader team helped keep me focused as I wrote. Kim Grant, Jesse Niemenen, Greg Saunders, Michael Doniger, Stella Sitt, Micah Chi, Ed Brzytwa, Patti Brennan, Tim Varan, Stasia Levin, Jason Grom, Patrick Wisneski, and Alison Southwick. Thank you.

The publishing team at New Degree Press could not have been more helpful in guiding me this past year. Your author-development process and coaching are extraordinary, and I sit in awe of your willingness and ability to consistently optimize every step of your work. Brian Bies, MacKenzie Finklea, Haley Newlin, and Kyra Ann Dawkins. Thank you.

The editing team did exceptional work that kept *The Optimizer* on schedule and on point. Thank you, Al Bagdonas, Max Abrams, and Kendra Kadam.

Thank you to my early supporters who purchased a first-time author's book, long before it was published. You've inspired me more than you'll ever know:

Gregg Everett, Richard Rath, Ben Carliner, Greg Saunders, Philip Holt, Robert Caruso, Philip McKeon, Shaveta Joshi, David Zicchinella, Brent Albright, William Moran, Daniel J. Gallagher, Matthew T. Gavora, Todd J. Thornley, Bryan Stein, Dennis Nolte, Stuart Chapman, Alison Davis, Rupa Athreya, John Kusturiss, James Robinson, Kim Grant, Peter Hanson, Katrina Hanson, Nicole Pretzel, Edward Brzytwa, Eric Horner, Stasia Levin, Greg P. Gerhartz, Ann Marie Selzer, Elizabeth Saunders, Robert Saunders, Jennifer Brown-Thornley, Tim Katusha, Lisa Whisenhunt, Eric Whisenhunt, Thomas Pryor, David Isaacson, Ryan Wertman, Daniel Blair, Rachel Blair,

Cady North, Scott Barker, Patti Brennan, Robert Thorsen, Patrick Sheridan, Jose Rovira, Joshua Broad, William Heinbockel, Prashant Malaviya, Lorna Lindquist, MJ Kim, Rebecca Myers, Joy Bochner, Rick Frank, Sharon Cohen, Dismas Locaria, Lala Balaoghlanova, Kevin Kelly, William M Beardsley, Rocky Granahan, Youssouf Diallo, Michael J. Doniger, Alan Panzer, Cynthia Bessette, Tara Scalia-Quilty, Rajeswari Ramanan, Kevin S. Gerry, Ivan Del Rio, Robert Darrow, Brian Austin, Christina Harris, Chris Hain, Maureen Truxton, Stefan Hull, Kimberly Mikec, Devin Benton, Michael Mardoian, Justin Goldstein, Neev Crane, Paul Ferraro, Stephen Gunter, Carolyn Boccaccio, Sheetal Jain, Lorraine Lods, Jay Therrien, Trish O'Connor, Rico Macaraeg, Ned Dane, Michael Gottesman, Jon L. Shea, Julie Matt, David Johnson, Elliott Smith, Alexandra Calderon, Emmanuel Kemiji, Joseph Hernandez, Zachary Eckert, Micah Eleazar, Judy Robinson, David Robinson, Carol Baugh, Dave Freedman, Meghan Gound, Travis Gound, Devinne Bravoco, Eric Koester, Graig Springer, Devon George, Ryan Wyatt, Brandon Waters, Michael Baratz, Nicholas Yaeger, Errol Iachini, Yasser El Shimy, Jason Grom, Benjamin Behrend, James Kirby, Alex Cope, Christopher M.N. Reid, Garrett Jones, Michael Castiglione, Mark Deschamp, Neil Sumilas, Giorgia Sumilas, Michael D. Stadnik, Alisa M. Parenti, Jerico Agdan, Dhruv Pateder, Krissy Pateder, Tim Koerper, Richard Hymes, Gregor Yuska, Jerry Mandzij, Paul Hooper, Katherine Mense, Lindsey Johnson, Michael Jaso, Sidney Baker, Elise Bacolas, Adrienne Hilts, Brooke & Keith Gensch, Doug Durham, Jessica Montgomery, Christy Felix, David Borrelli, Jerry Brace, Lawrence Forlenza, Jessica Fernandez, Carter Loetz, William McNamara, Michelle Borre, Alison Weiss, Kasra Ferdows, Zack DiLeo

Sean Connolly, Collin Misquith, Spencer Mindlin, Jay Gentry, Nicole Arwood, Susan Burton, William Raynor, Jr., E. Abraham, Charles Jonas, Jennifer Dalton, Mike Malloy, Kate Hyun, Tim Varan, Beatriz Luna Vida, Christine Steel, John Scott Napier, Daniel Lee, Carlo Mahfouz, Julie Diaz-Asper, Kevin Lusinski, Brian Levitt, Brian Munson, Chris Rainey, Andrew Chonofsky, Eileen Reyna, Edward Nini, Stephen Flippin, Cameron Dunford, Patrick Wisneski, Tatiana Koleva, Tania Galarza, David Thomas, Fernando Del Llano, Jesse Nieminen, David Mazza, David Yergin-Doniger, Brian Kiley, Joseph Moran, Brian Thorp, Daniel Stein, Jimmy Mugno, Ian Roche, LeaAnna Hartman, Brandon Ripley, Tiffany Freeland, Peter Winters, Wesley Vance, Michael Guman, Sahil Rahman, Michael Haas, Roberto Impeduglia, Ben Stewart, Manpreet Singh Anand, Micah McDonald, Frank Castellanos, Andrew Snow, Kamal Bhatia, Ken Brodsky, Matt Dudek, Mary Kertz-Jones, Wendy and Joseph Ehrlich, and Elizabeth Kerr.

* * *

My deepest gratitude and thanks goes to my family.

Thank you to my parents, Robert and Elizabeth Saunders, for teaching me the value of education and inspiring me to never stop learning.

This author journey would not have been possible without the support and understanding of my wife, Dina, and our two young boys, John and Joe. Nothing makes hours of writing and revisions quickly fade away like any one of their smiles.

Dina: you helped me solidify and clarify my thoughts on so many occasions and navigate dozens of bouts with writer's block, and for this guidance I am especially grateful. I could not have written this book without you.

John and Joe: I hope this book inspires both of you to continue to create, never stop wondering how to improve, and to be humble and thoughtful leaders, which I'm sure you will one day be.

Appendix

Introduction

"20 Largest Companies by Market Capitalization." *The Online Investor*, Updated September 13, 2020. https://www.theonlineinvestor.com/large_caps/.

Anthony, Scott D., S. Patrick Viguerie, Evan I. Schwartz, and John Van Landeghem. "Corporate Longevity Forecast: Creative Destruction Is Accelerating." Innosight Strategy and Innovation at Huron, February 2018. https://www.innosight.com/insight/creative-destruction/.

Assis, Claudia. "Macy's to Leave the S&P 500 Index." *MarketWatch*, March 31, 2020. https://www.marketwatch.com/story/macys-to-leave-the-sp-500-index-2020-03-31.

Barrett, Eamon. "Meituan Dianping: China's 'Amazon for Services' Confirms IPO Plans." *Fortune,* September 11, 2018. https://fortune.com/2018/09/11/meituan-ipo-china-tech-slump/.

Lahiri, Tripti, and John Dextrixhe. "China's Favorite Food Delivery Service Is Now Worth More than Its Biggest Internet Search Firm." *Quartz*, June 24, 2019. https://qz.com/1648807/bat-no-more-meituan-dianping-is-now-worth-more-than-baidu/.

Robinson, Jonathan, Cheskie Rosenzweig, Aaron J. Moss, and Leib Litman. "Tapped out or Barely Tapped? Recommendations for How to Harness the Vast and Largely Unused Potential of the Mechanical Turk Participant Pool." *PLOS ONE* 14, no. 12 (December 16, 2019): e0226394. https://doi.org/10.1371/journal.pone.0226394.

Schwartz, Oscar. "Untold History of AI: How Amazon's Mechanical Turkers Got Squeezed Inside the Machine." *IEEE Spectrum*, April 22, 2019. https://spectrum.ieee.org/tech-talk/tech-history/dawn-of-electronics/untold-history-of-ai-mechanical-turk-revisited-tktkt.

Chapter 1

"100 Years Since the Purchase of The Waterloo Boy." *AgWeb*, Accessed September 15, 2020. https://www.agweb.com/article/100-years-since-the-purchase-of-the-waterloo-boy.

Atkinson, Robert. "Resistance is Futile." Interview by Ramtin Arablouei and Rund Abdelfatah. *Throughline*, NPR, April 25, 2019. Audio, 37:01. https://www.npr.org/2019/04/23/716521520/resistance-is-futile.

Blitz, Matt. "Inside the Car Company That's Resurrecting the DeLorean." *Popular Mechanics*, January 18, 2019.

https://www.popularmechanics.com/cars/a25938392/
inside-delorean-motor-company/.

Brown, Aaron. "GM EV1 History." *Business Insider*, Accessed
September 23, 2020. https://www.businessinsider.com/
gm-ev1-history-2016-3#when-gm-began-recollecting-ev1s-
for-demolishing-many-enthusiasts-came-together-to-give-
their-piece-of-mind-and-attempt-to-put-a-stop-to-the-
crushing-of-their-beloved-electric-cars-12.

Bureau, US Census. "Eleventh Census - Volume 5. Statistics
of Agriculture in the US." The United States Census Bureau.
Accessed September 15, 2020. https://www.census.gov/library/
publications/1895/dec/volume-5.html.

"China, India Among Nations to Dominate Global
Growth in 2024." *Bloomberg*, Accessed September 15, 2020.
https://www.bloomberg.com/news/articles/2019-10-19/
which-20-countries-will-dominate-global-growth-in-2024.

Consumer Electronics Show. "John Deere 8RX Tractor."
Accessed August 15, 2020. https://www.ces.tech/Innova-
tion-Awards/Honorees/2020/Honorees/J/John-Deere-8RX-
Tractor.aspx.

Conference on Research in Income and Wealth, National
Bureau of Economic Research, and Economic History Association (U.S.). *Output, Employment, and Productivity in the
United States after 1800*. New York: National Bureau of Economic Research; distributed by Columbia University Press,
1966. http://books.google.com/books?id=77MSAQAAMAAJ.

Davis, Joshua. "How Elon Musk Turned Tesla into the Car Company of the Future." *Wired*, September 27, 2010. https://www.wired.com/2010/09/ff-tesla/.

Editors, History. "John Froelich, Inventor of the Gas-Powered Tractor, Is Born." *History*, Accessed September 15, 2020. https://www.history.com/this-day-in-history/john-froelich-inventor-of-the-gas-powered-tractor-is-born.

"Founder John Deere | Past Leaders | John Deere US." Accessed September 15, 2020. https://www.deere.com/en/our-company/about-john-deere/past-leaders/john-deere/.

"How Much Did the First Light Bulb Cost?" Accessed September 15, 2020. https://www.reference.com/history/much-did-first-light-bulb-cost-a86747b199434c25.

"Inflation Calculator | Find US Dollar's Value from 1913-2020." Accessed September 15, 2020. https://www.usinflationcalculator.com/.

"John Deere Technology Innovation Center - Research Park." Accessed September 15, 2020. https://researchpark.illinois.edu/tenant_directory/john-deere-technology-innovation-center/.

Kiger, Patrick J. "6 Inventions by Thomas Edison That Took the World by Storm." *History*. Accessed September 15, 2020. https://www.history.com/news/thomas-edison-inventions.

Killa, Sweta. "John Deere Q2 Results Put Agribusiness ETFs in Focus." Accessed September 15, 2020. https://finance.yahoo.com/news/john-deere-q2-results-put-151003798.html.

Landers, Jackson. "Did John Deere's Best Invention Spark a Revolution or an Environmental Disaster?" Smithsonian Magazine. Accessed September 14, 2020. https://www.smithsonianmag.com/smithsonian-institution/did-john-deeres-best-invention-spark-revolution-or-environmental-disaster-180957080/.

Lelyveld, Michael. "China Unveils New Strategy for Economic Growth." *Radio Free Asia*, August 21, 2020. https://www.rfa.org/english/commentaries/energy_watch/economy-08212020094605.html.

"Lessons in the How: Deere Visits Henry Ford | The John Deere Journal." Accessed September 15, 2020. https://johndeerejournal.com/2018/08/lessons-in-the-how-deere-visits-henry-ford/.

Locke, Taylor. "Elon Musk: 'I Really Didn't Want to Be CEO of Tesla'—Here's How He Says It Happened." *CNBC*, January 30, 2020. https://www.cnbc.com/2020/01/30/elon-musk-i-really-didnt-want-to-be-ceo-of-tesla.html.

Martin, Gary. "'Necessity Is the Mother of Invention'—the Meaning and Origin of This Phrase." *Phrasefinder*. Accessed September 23, 2020. https://www.phrases.org.uk/meanings/necessity-is-the-mother-of-invention.html.

Menlo Park Museum. "Thomas Edison and Menlo Park." Accessed July 13, 2020. https://www.menloparkmuseum.org/history.

Merriam-Webster, s.v. "innovation." Accessed July 12, 2020. https://www.merriam-webster.com/dictionary/innovation.

Palermo, Elizabeth. "Who Invented the Light Bulb?" *Live Science*, Accessed September 15, 2020. https://www.livescience.com/43424-who-invented-the-light-bulb.html.

Ramey, Jay. "The First Tesla Roadster: A Look Back at the Early Adopter's Electric Car." *Autoweek*, November 27, 2017. http://autoweek.com/news/green-cars/a1835876/first-tesla-roadster-look-back-early-adopters-electric-car/.

Reed, Eric. "History of Tesla: Timeline and Facts." *TheStreet*. Accessed September 15, 2020. https://www.thestreet.com/technology/history-of-tesla-15088992.

"Tesla Battery Day Teaser, Extortion Sting Operation, Octovalve Updates, Lucid Air Battery - YouTube." Accessed September 15, 2020. https://www.youtube.com/watch?v=JnpgtsLfPoY&t=300.

"Tesla: Martin Eberhard Calls Tesla His 'Baby,' Talks about Being Ousted from Company's Board" *The Economic Times*, Accessed September 15, 2020. https://economictimes.indiatimes.com/magazines/panache/martin-eberhard-calls-tesla-his-baby-talks-about-being-ousted-from-companys-board/articleshow/68211761.cms.

Tesla Corporation. "Tesla's Mission Is to Accelerate the World's Transition to Sustainable Energy." Accessed August 17, 2020. https://www.tesla.com/about.

Tesla Corporation. "Upgrades." Accessed August 17, 2020. https://www.tesla.com/support/upgrades.

Tesla Daily. "Tesla Battery Day Teaser, Extortion Sting Operation, Octovalve Updates, Lucid Air Battery." August 27, 2020. Video, 11:01. https://www.youtube.com/watch?v=JnpgtsLfPoY&t=300.

"Tesla Model 3 Dominates US Premium-Class Small & Midsize Car Market — 23 percent of 2019 Sales*." Accessed September 15, 2020. https://cleantechnica.com/2020/01/18/tesla-model-3-dominates-us-premium-class-small-midsize-car-market-24-of-2019-sales/.

"Tesla's Betting You'll Pay $9,000 for a Software Upgrade." Accessed September 15, 2020. https://www.bloomberg.com/graphics/2016-tesla-model-s/.

"The Steel Plow." Accessed September 15, 2020. http://www.iwest.k12.il.us/schools/thawville/projects/1800/index_017.html.

Thomas Edison Quotes." *GoodReads*, Accessed May 20, 2020. https://www.goodreads.com/author/quotes/3091287. Thomas A Edison.

"Top 10 Best-Selling Plug-In Electric Cars in U.S. - 2019 Edition." *InsideEVs*, Accessed September 15, 2020. https://insideevs.com/news/392375/top-10-electric-cars-sales-us-2019/.

U.S. Department of Energy. "Timeline: History of the Electric Car." Accessed August 16, 2020. https://www.energy.gov/timeline/timeline-history-electric-car.

Visual Capitalist. "The History of Tesla in 5 Minutes." January 15, 2019. Video, 5:51. https://www.youtube.com/watch?v=pQiT2U5E9tI.

"Want to Save the World? Start Thinking like Thomas Edison." *Real Leaders,* October 17, 2015. https://real-leaders.com/want-save-world-start-thinking-like-thomas-edison/.

Winfield, Barry. "Tested: 1997 General Motors EV1 Proves to Be the Start of Something Big." *Car and Driver,* June 24, 2020. https://www.caranddriver.com/reviews/a32944084/tested-1997-general-motors-ev1-proves-to-be-the-start-of-something-big/.

Chapter 2

Atkinson, Robert. "Resistance is Futile." Interview by Ramtin Arablouei and Rund Abdelfatah. *Throughline,* NPR, April 25, 2019. Audio, 37:01. https://www.npr.org/2019/04/23/716521520/resistance-is-futile.

Adamczyk, Alicia. "Index funds are more popular than ever— here's why they're a smart investment." *CNBC,* September 19, 2019. https://www.cnbc.com/2019/09/19/why-index-funds-are-a-smart-investment.html

Bucy, Michael, Adrian Finlayson, Greg Kelly and Chris Moye. "The 'How' Of Transformation." *McKinsey,* May 9, 2016. https://www.mckinsey.com/industries/retail/our-insights/the-how-of-transformation.

Cboe Corporation. "VIX Index Charts & Data." Accessed August 17, 2020. http://www.cboe.com/vix.

Chart Comparing CBOE Volatility Index versus ICI Money Market Assets 1/5/90 to 8/14/20, via Bloomberg LP, Accessed August 14, 2020.

Chrystal, Paul. "A Drink for the Devil: 8 Facts about the History of Coffee." *History Extra,* May 28, 2019. https://www.historyextra.com/period/medieval/history-coffee-facts-discovery-use-drink-social-revolution/.

Dannemiller, Doug and Sean Collins. "2020 investment management outlook." *Deloitte Insights,* December 3, 2019. https://www2.deloitte.com/us/en/insights/industry/financial-services/financial-services-industry-outlooks/investment-management-industry-outlook.html.

Filz, Gretchen. "The Devil's Drink: How the Pope Cheated Hell by "Baptizing" Coffee." *Get-Fed,* November 15, 2018. https://www.getfed.com/devils-drink-how-pope-clement-made-coffee-catholic-6234/.

Glazer, Robert. "'Command and Control' Leadership is Dead. Here's What's Taking Its Place." *Inc.,* August 12 ,2019. https://www.inc.com/robert-glazer/command-control-leadership-is-dead-heres-whats-taking-its-place.html.

Godin, Benoit. "'Innovation: The History of a Category." *Project on the Intellectual History of Innovation,* Working Paper no. 1 (2008): 35. http://www.csiic.ca/PDF/IntellectualNo1.pdf.

Godin, Benoit. "καινοτομία: An Old Word for a New World, or The De-Contestation of a Political and Contested

Concept." *Project on the Intellectual History of Innovation,* Working Paper no. 9. (2011): 39. http://www.csiic.ca/PDF/Old-New.pdf.

Godin, Benoit. "'Meddle Not with Them That Are Given to Change': Innovation as Evil." *Project on the Intellectual History Innovation,* Working Paper no. 6 (2010): 12-27. http://www.csiic.ca/PDF/IntellectualNo6.pdf.

Harter, Jim. "Why Some Leaders Have Their Employees' Trust, and Some Don't." *Gallup,* June 13, 2019. https://www.gallup.com/workplace/258197/why-leaders-employees-trust-don.aspx.

Holmes, Ryan. "The Elephant and the Rope: One Mental Trick to Unlock Your Growth." *Inc.,* January 30, 2017. https://www.inc.com/ryan-holmes/the-elephant-and-the-rope-one-mental-trick-to-unlock-your-growth.html.

Kessler, David. "The Five Stages of Grief." *Grief,* Accessed May 4, 2020. https://grief.com/the-five-stages-of-grief/.

Moss Kanter, Rosabeth. "Ten Reasons People Resist Change." *HBR,* September 25, 2012. https://hbr.org/2012/09/ten-reasons-people-resist-chang#:~:text=Loss%20of%20control.,change%20coming%20from%20someone%20else.

Pacher, Sigurd. "Innovation and Entrepreneurship - The Austrian Economist Joseph A. Schumpeter." *Austria.* Accessed September 23, 2020. https://www.austria.org/austrianinformation/2015/3/27/innovation-and-entrepreneurship-the-austrian-economist-joseph-a-schumpeter.

Pound, Jesse. "There's Nearly $5 Trillion Parked in Money Markets as Many Investors Are Still Afraid of Stocks." *CNBC*, June 22, 2020. https://www.cnbc.com/2020/06/22/theres-nearly-5-trillion-parked-in-money-markets-as-many-investors-are-still-afraid-of-stocks.html.

Sahadi, Jeanne. "Vanguard's John Bogle Dies at 89. Father of the Index Fund, He Brought Investing to the Masses." *CNN*, January 17, 2019. https://www.cnn.com/2019/01/16/investing/john-bogle-obituary/index.html.

Lim, Paul. "Investors Put Index Funds, if Not Their Theory, Into Practice." *LA Times*, September 26, 1999. https://www.latimes.com/archives/la-xpm-1999-sep-26-fi-14320-story.html.

Vanguard. "Not all index funds are created equal." Accessed August 15, 2020. https://investor.vanguard.com/index-funds/.

Collie, Bob, Marisa Hall, Tim Hodgson, Roger Urwin and Liang Yin. "The world's largest fund managers - 2019." *Thinking Ahead Institute*, 2019. https://www.thinkingaheadinstitute.org/en/Library/Public/Research-and-Ideas/2019/10/P_I_500_2019_Survey.

Winch Ph. D, Guy. "10 Signs That You Might Have Fear of Failure." *Psychology Today*, June 18, 2018. https://www.psychologytoday.com/us/blog/the-squeaky-wheel/201306/10-signs-you-might-have-fear-failure.

Chapter 3

Amadeo, Kimberly. "Irrational Exuberance, Its Quotes, Dangers, and Examples." *The Balance*, May 30, 2019. https://www.thebalance.com/irrational-exuberance-quotes-dangers-and-examples-3305937.

Andrew, Owen. "The History and Evolution of the Smartphone: 1992-2018." *Text Request*, August 28, 2018. https://www.textrequest.com/blog/history-evolution-smartphone/.

Blank, Steve. "Why the Lean Start-Up Changes Everything." *HBR*, May 2013. https://hbr.org/2013/05/why-the-lean-start-up-changes-everything.

Bryan, Kathy. "Kozmo: Bad Idea or Ahead of Its Time?" *Digital Marketing News*, August 14, 2018. https://insights.digitalmediasolutions.com/articles/kozmo-com-bad-idea-or-ahead-of-its-time.

Ciccolela, Tom, Mark McCaffrey, Greg Vlahos, Leo Bley, David Silverman, Danny Wallace and Gary Meltzer. "PwC MoneyTree Report." *PwC MoneyTree*, Q1 2020. https://www.pwc.com/us/en/industries/technology/moneytree.html.

Coffman, K.G. and Andrew Odlyzko. "The Size and Growth Rate of the Internet." *First Monday*, 1998. https://firstmonday.org/ojs/index.php/fm/article/view/620/541.

"The 50 Worst Internet Startup Fails of All Time." *Complex*, October 18, 2012. https://www.complex.com/pop-culture/2012/10/the-50-worst-internet-startup-fails-of-all-time/.

Gallagher, Fergal. "The Mysterious Origins of The Term Silicon Alley Revealed." *Built In NYC*, November 4, 2015. https://www.builtinnyc.com/2015/10/12/where-exactly-or-was-silicon-alley.

Leibovich, Mark. "Nasdaq Hits 4000 for 84 percent Gain in '99." *Washington Post*, December 30, 1999. https://www.washingtonpost.com/archive/politics/1999/12/30/nasdaq-hits-4000-for-84-gain-in-99/0cfa8bee-658b-4948-90ca-dc2f-da4abfa0/.

McCullough, Brian. "A Revealing Look at The Dot-Com Bubble of 2000—And How It Shapes Our Lives Today." *Ideas. TED.Com*, December 4, 2018. https://ideas.ted.com/an-eye-opening-look-at-the-dot-com-bubble-of-2000-and-how-it-shapes-our-lives-today/.

Ries, Eric. "Creating the Lean Startup." *Inc.*, October 2011. https://www.inc.com/magazine/201110/eric-ries-usability-testing-product-development.html.

Ries, Eric. "The Lean Startup Methodology." *The Lean Startup*, Accessed May 16, 2020. http://theleanstartup.com/principles.

"The 50 Worst Internet Startup Fails of All Time." *Complex*, October 18, 2012. https://www.complex.com/pop-culture/2012/10/the-50-worst-internet-startup-fails-of-all-time/.

VoiceHive, LLC. "Here's What Our Clients Have to Say." Accessed May 13, 2020. https://www.voicehive.com/testimonials.

Writer, Staff. "What Is Lean." *Lean*, Accessed May 15, 2020. https://www.lean.org/whatslean/.

Zider, Bob. "How Venture Capital Works." *HBR*, November-December 1998. https://hbr.org/1998/11/how-venture-capital-works.

Chapter 4
Chamorro-Premuzic, Tomas, and Cindy Gallop. "7 Leadership Lessons Men Can Learn from Women." April 1, 2020. https://hbr.org/2020/04/7-leadership-lessons-men-can-learn-from-women.

Downey, Daniel. "Barron's Financial Advisor Hall of Fame." *Barron's*, October 25, 2019. https://www.barrons.com/articles/barrons-financial-advisor-hall-of-fame-51572028751.

Garmhausen, Steve. "Women Make Great Financial Advisors. So Why Aren't There More?" *Barron's*, Updated June 8, 2019. https://www.barrons.com/articles/women-make-great-financial-advisors-so-why-arent-there-more-51559952001.

Goleman, Daniel. *HBR'S 10 MUST READS: On Emotional Intelligence*. Boston: Harvard Business Review Press, 2015.

Loyd, Sam. *Sam Loyd's Cyclopedia of 5000 Puzzles Tricks and Conundrums: With Answers*. New York: The Lamb Publishing Company, 1914. https://archive.org/details/CyclopediaOfPuzzlesLoyd/page/n191/mode/2up.

Maranjian, Selena. "15 Years of Fooling Around." *Fool.com*, Updated April 5, 2017. https://www.fool.com/investing/general/2008/10/15/15-years-of-fooling-around.aspx

Staff, CNBC. "Timeline: AOL through the Years." *CNBC*, May 12, 2015. https://www.cnbc.com/2015/05/12/timeline-aol-through-the-years.html.

TED Talks. "Teresa Amabile: The Progress Principle." October 12, 2011. Video, 18:36. https://www.youtube.com/watch?v=XD6N8bsjOEE.

Wofford, Benjamin. "The Motley Fool Is 25 This Year. Here's How They Changed the Way America Invests." *Washingtonian*, April 1, 2019. https://www.washingtonian.com/2019/04/01/the-motley-fool-is-25-this-year-heres-how-they-changed-the-way-america-invests/.

Chapter 5

Brassey, Jacqueline, Nick van Dam and Katie Coates. "Seven Essential Elements of a Lifelong-Learning Mind-Set." *McKinsey*, February 19, 2019. https://www.mckinsey.com/business-functions/organization/our-insights/seven-essential-elements-of-a-lifelong-learning-mind-set.

Paul, Shale. "The Top 10 Characteristics of Problem Solvers." *Strategic Searches*, September 24, 2017. http://www.strategicsearches.com/2017/09/24/top-10-characteristics-problem-solvers/.

"The Hidden Habits of Great Problem Solvers." *Korn Ferry Advance*, Accessed April 12, 2020. https://www.kfadvance.com/articles/become-better-problem-solver.

Webb, Kevin. "The Best-Selling Video Game of Every Year, from 1995 to 2019." *Business Insider*, December 25, 2019. https://www.businessinsider.com/best-selling-video-game-every-year-2018-11#2007-guitar-hero-iii-legends-of-rock-playstation-2-playstation-3-xbox-xbox-360-wii-microsoft-windows-mac-os-x-13.

Chapter 6

Anzilotti, Eillie, Jeff Beer, Laura Bell, Joe Berkowitz, Jill Bernstein, Adam Bluestein, Morgan Clendaniel et al. "The World's 50 Most Innovative Companies 2019." *Fast Company*, March/April 2019. https://www.fastcompany.com/most-innovative-companies/2019.

CB Insights Research. "The Top 100 Venture Capitalists." *CB Insights*, March 31, 2019. https://www.cbinsights.com/research/top-venture-capital-partners/.

Chen, Lulu, David Ramli and Peter Elstrom. "The World's Greatest Delivery Empire." *Forbes*, March 28, 2019. https://www.bloomberg.com/features/2019-meituan-china-delivery-empire/.

China Power (blog). "How Well-Off Is China's Middle Class?" Updated August 26, 2020. Accessed August 27, 2020. https://chinapower.csis.org/china-middle-class/#:~:text=Since%20the%20early%202000s%2C%20China's,this%20growth%20is%20particularly%20noteworthy.

Epstein, Gady. "The Cloner." *Forbes*, April 28, 2011. https://www.forbes.com/global/2011/0509/companies-wang-xing-china-groupon-friendster-cloner.html#7df1977755a6.

Food Navigator USA. "Which States Are Net Producers versus Net Consumers?" Updated November 3, 2017. https://www.foodnavigator-usa.com/Article/2017/11/03/Which-states-are-net-producers-versus-net-consumers#.

Fortune. "Fortune 500." *Fortune*, 2019. https://fortune.com/fortune500/2019/search/.

Iskyan, Kim. "China's Middle Class Is Exploding." *Business Insider*, August 27, 2016. https://www.businessinsider.com/chinas-middle-class-is-exploding-2016-8.

Laboe, Daniel. "Alibaba Vs. Amazon: Who Will Take Over the World First." *Yahoo Finance*, April 8, 2019. https://finance.yahoo.com/news/alibaba-vs-amazon-over-world-194807613.html.

Lee, Emma. "There Are No Food Delivery Winners." *Technode*, April 29, 2020. https://technode.com/2020/04/29/there-are-no-food-delivery-winners/.

Lee, Emma and Nicole Jao. "Meituan Faces Challenge from Alipay on Its Home Turf." *Technode*, April 1, 2020. https://technode.com/2020/04/01/meituan-faces-challenge-from-alipay-on-its-home-turf/.

Lahiri, Tripti and John Dextrixhe. "China's Favorite Food Delivery Service Is Now Worth More Than Its Biggest Internet

Search Firm." *Quartz*, June 24, 2019. https://qz.com/1648807/
bat-no-more-meituan-dianping-is-now-worth-more-than-
baidu/.

Lidsky, David. "The 2 Most Innovative Companies in the World Today Are Changing How Hundreds of Millions of Asian Consumers Buy Food, Book
Hotels, and (A Lot) More." *Fast Company*, February 19, 2019. https://www.fastcompany.com/90298866/
meituan-grab-most-innovative-companies-2019.

Marklew, Tim. "Michigan's Grand Rapids Was Once
Known as Furniture City." *Culture Trip*, May 7, 2018. https://
theculturetrip.com/north-america/usa/michigan/articles/
michigans-grand-rapids-was-once-known-as-furniture-city/.

Mikhailova, Valeriia. "Food Delivery in China: A Rapidly
Expanding Tech Battleground." *China Economy* (blog). *Daxueconsulting*, March 11, 2020. https://daxueconsulting.com/
food-delivery-online/.

Miller, Kenneth. "Is China Winning the Innovation
Race?" *Leapsmag*, June 19, 2018. https://leapsmag.com/
is-china-winning-the-innovation-race/.

Morgan, Blake. "The 10 Most Customer-Obsessed Companies in 2018." *Forbes*, February 15, 2018. https://www.forbes.
com/sites/blakemorgan/2018/02/15/the-10-most-customer-
obsessed-companies-in-2018/#59d7bad46ba1.

Morgan Stanley Corporation. "Can Food Delivery Apps Deliver Profits for Investors?" February 21, 2020. https://www.morganstanley.com/ideas/food-delivery-app-profits.

Oster, Shai and Yunan Zhang. "A Chinese Startup's Big Ambition: Amazon for Services." *The Information*, March 27, 2018. https://www.theinformation.com/articles/a-chinese-startups-big-ambition-amazon-for-services.

Prisco, Jacopo. "Keep Calm: The Story behind the UK's Most Famous Poster Design." *CNN Style*, November 1, 2017. https://www.cnn.com/style/article/keep-calm-poster/index.html.

PR Newswire. "Meituan to Invest rmb11 Billion to Support Merchant Development." *PR Newswire*, January 23, 2019. https://www.prnewswire.com/news-releases/meituan-to-invest-rmb11-billion-to-support-merchant-development-300782802.html.

Schneider, Jordan. "Meituan's CEO Wang Xing at 40, Without Doubts." *ChinaTalk*, June 21, 2019. https://chinatalk.substack.com/p/meituans-ceo-wang-xing-at-40-without.

Spero, Josh and Nian Liu. "Meituan Dianping Shows Route to Food Delivery Profits." *Financial Times*, December 15, 2019. https://www.ft.com/content/7b566b44-1cda-11ea-9186-7348c2f183af.

Vashishtha, Yashica. "Wang Xing: Chinese Billionaire Businessman & the Founder of Meituan." *Your Tech Story*, April 6, 2019. http://www.yourtechstory.com/2019/04/06/wang-xing-chinese-billionaire-businessman-founder-meituan/.

Wang, Yue. "China's Meituan, Dianping Merge to Create a Mega Online-to-Offline Service Platform." *Forbes*, October 8, 2015. https://www.forbes.com/sites/ywang/2015/10/08/chinas-meituan-dianping-merges-to-create-a-mega-online-to-offline-service-platform/#fbf42123e287.

Yang, Yang. "Meituan Makes Robust Stock Debut in Hong Kong." *China Daily*, September 21, 2018. https://www.chinadaily.com.cn/a/201809/21/WS5ba499faa310c4cc775e7947.html.

Yang, Yingzhi. "China's Meituan Dianping Pushes Its Short Delivery Service to More Customers in Search for Profit." South China Morning Post, May 7, 2019. https://www.scmp.com/tech/apps-social/article/3009126/chinas-meituan-dianping-pushes-its-short-delivery-service-more.

Yin, Carol. "Meituan Hotels Surpassed Ctrip to Lead the Online Hotel Booking Industry in q2 2018." *Pandaily*, September 3, 2018. https://pandaily.com/meituan-hotels-surpassed-ctrip-to-lead-the-online-hotel-booking-industry-in-q2-2018/.

Zhou, Kevin. "Meituan CEO Talked about Relationships with Bat." *Pandaily*, June 28, 2017. https://pandaily.com/interview-with-wang-xing-too-many-people-focus-on-the-borderline-and-neglect-the-core-of-their-business/.

Zhu, Julie. "China's Meituan Dianping to focus on domestic market after $4.4 billion Hong Kong IPO." *Reuters*, September 6, 2018. https://www.reuters.com/article/us-meituan-ipo/chinas-meituan-dianping-to-focus-on-domestic-market-after-4-4-billion-hong-kong-ipo-idUSKCN1LM1DE.

Chapter 7

Briscoe, Stacy. "Top 10 U.S. Wine Distributors." Wines & Vines, September 2018. https://winesvinesanalytics.com/features/article/202690/Top-10-US-Wine-Distributors.

Burton, Jonathan. "Morningstar Plans $100 Million IPO." *MarketWatch*, May 6, 2004. https://www.marketwatch.com/story/fund-tracking-firm-morningstar-files-for-100-mln-ipo.

Business Wire. "May 1st Marks 30th Anniversary of Brokerage Commission Deregulation." April 28, 2005. https://www.businesswire.com/news/home/20050922005531/en/1st-Marks-30th-Anniversary-Brokerage-Commission-Deregulation

Charles Schwab Corporation. "Our Purpose Drives Our Every Action." Who We Are. Accessed June 16, 2020. https://www.aboutschwab.com/who-we-are.

Charles Schwab Corporation. "1973-1986: Leading an Investor Revolution." Company History. Accessed June 15, 2020. https://www.aboutschwab.com/history.

Charles Schwab Corporation. "1987-1994: Expanding Service and Access." Company History. Accessed June 15, 2020. https://www.aboutschwab.com/history.

Charles Schwab Corporation. "2001–2007: Banking on Added Value." Company History. Accessed June 15, 2020. https://www.aboutschwab.com/history.

Charles Schwab Corporation. "Our Results Speak for Themselves." Who We Are. Accessed June 16, 2020. https://www.aboutschwab.com/who-we-are.

Charles Schwab Corporation. "Sneak Peek: Charles Schwab's New Memoir." Personal Finance & Planning. August 23, 2019. https://www.schwab.com/resource-center/insights/content/sneak-peek-charles-schwabs-new-memoir-invested.

Charles Schwab Corporation. "We Are Champions of Investors and Those Who Serve Them." Who We Are. Accessed June 16, 2020. https://www.aboutschwab.com/who-we-are.

Charles Schwab. Interview by David Rubenstein. *The David Rubenstein Show*. February 20, 2020. https://www.bloomberg.com/news/videos/2020-02-20/the-david-rubenstein-show-charles-schwab-video.

Child Mind Institute. "A Conversation with Charles Schwab on Struggling and Succeeding with Dyslexia." March 12, 2019. Video, 56:53. https://www.youtube.com/watch?v=tdvMq-Ko7zY.

CNBC Television. "Investing Legend Charles Schwab Discusses the Market, His Career and His New Book, 'Invested: Changing Forever the Way Americans Invest,' with CNBC's Bob Pisani." October 7, 2019. Video, 18:55. https://www.youtube.com/watch?v=3N_oewzG324.

Collins, Sean, Rochelle Antoniewicz, Sarah Holden and Judy Steenstra. Investment Company Institute. *2020 Investment Company Fact Book: A Review of Trends and Activities in the*

Investment Company Industry. 60th Edition. 2020. https://
www.ici.org/pdf/2020_factbook.pdf.

Encyclopedia.com. "Pioneer Discount Broker." Updated
September 24, 2020. https://www.encyclopedia.com/
social-sciences-and-law/economics-business-and-labor/
businesses-and-occupations/charles-schwab-corp-o.

Federal Reserve Board. Federal Reserve Bulletin. *Mutual
Funds and the U.S. Equity Market*, by Eric M. Engen, Andreas
Lehnert and Richard Kehoe. December 2000. https://www.
federalreserve.gov/pubs/bulletin/2000/1200lead.pdf.

Funding Universe. "The Charles Schwab Corporation
History." Company History. Accessed June 15, 2020.
http://www.fundinguniverse.com/company-histories/
the-charles-schwab-corporation-history/.

Ghost Horse Wines. "Our Wines." Accessed May 19, 2020.
https://www.ghosthorseworld.com/Wines.

Goday, Maria. "The Judgment of Paris: The Blind Taste
Test That Decanted the Wine World." *NPR*, May 24, 2016.
https://www.npr.org/sections/thesalt/2016/05/24/479163882/
the-judgment-of-paris-the-blind-taste-test-that-decanted-
the-wine-world.

Gray, W. Blake. "Napa Pricing Risks Alienating Consumers."
Wine-Searcher, January 23, 2020. https://www.wine-searcher.
com/m/2020/01/napa-pricing-risks-alienating-consumers.

Hur, Johnson. "History of Online Stock Trading." *Be Businessed.* Accessed September 9, 2020. https://bebusinessed. com/history/history-of-online-stock-trading/.

Inc. "From May Day to Heydays." October 1, 2019. https:// www.inc.com/charles-schwab/from-may-day-to-heydays. html.

Internet Live Stats. "Total Number of Websites." Accessed September 9, 2020. https://www.internetlivestats.com/ total-number-of-websites/.

Investment Master Class (blog). "Learning from Charles Schwab." April 10, 2020. Accessed September 1, 2020. http://mastersinvest.com/newblog/2020/2/3/ learning-from-charles-schwab.

Keppel, Bruce. "Feud Shines Spotlight on Joseph Gallo." *LA Times,* August 10, 1986. https://www.latimes.com/archives/ la-xpm-1986-08-10-fi-2357-story.html#:~:text=On%20 Joseph%20Gallo's%20discharge%20from,and%20the%20 Gallo%20Cattle%20Co.

LaFrance, Adrienne. "A Search for the Zombie Websites of 1995." *The Atlantic,* April 21, 2017. https://www.theatlantic. com/technology/archive/2017/04/a-search-for-the-zombie- websites-of-1995/523848/.

Lehnert and Richard Kehoe. December 2000. https://www. federalreserve.gov/pubs/bulletin/2000/1200lead.pdf.

Leve, Jeff. "Complete Napa Valley California Wine History from Early 1800s to Today." The Wine Cellar Insider, Accessed May 22, 2020. https://www.thewinecellarinsider. com/california-wine/california-wine-history-from-early-plantings-in-1800s-to-today/.

Sablik, Tim. "Recession of 1981–82." *Federal Reserve History.* November 22, 2013. https://www.federalreservehistory.org/ essays/recession_of_1981_82.

Sullivan, Paul. "Winemaking Lures the Wealthy, but Not with Profits." *NY Times*, May 25, 2012. https://www.nytimes. com/2012/05/26/your-money/winemaking-lures-the-wealthy-but-not-with-profits.html.

"The David Rubenstein Show: Charles Schwab." *Bloomberg*, February 20, 2020. https://www. bloomberg.com/news/videos/2020-02-20/ the-david-rubenstein-show-charles-schwab-video.

Tomczyk, Fred. "Lessons from 40 Years of Mayday on Wall Street: Column." *USA Today*, May 1, 2015. https://www. usatoday.com/story/opinion/2015/05/01/mayday-anniversary-wall-street-investment-column/26463281/.

U.S. Census Bureau. "Household Money Income in 1975 and Selected Social and Economic Characteristics of Households." Publications, Briefs and Reports from Census Bureau Experts, 1975, table A. Accessed May 28, 2020. https://www.census.gov/ library/publications/1977/demo/p60-104.html.

Waggoner, John. "Icons: Schwab Still Roots for the Small Investor." *USA Today,* April 11, 2013. https://www.usa-today.com/story/money/personalfinance/2013/04/11/schwab-icon-of-the-small-investor/2070573/.

Walt Disney World. "Disney Private VIP Tours." Accessed May 19, 2020. https://disneyworld.disney.go.com/events-tours/private-vip-tours/.

Walt Disney World. "Standard Theme Park Ticket in 2020." Accessed May 19, 2020. https://disneyworld.disney.go.com/admission/tickets/.

Ward, Bill. "Minnesota Native Changed the Course of Napa Wines." Diamond Creek Vineyards, Accessed May 20, 2020. https://www.diamondcreekvineyards.com/history.html.

Weed, Augustus. "Napa Winemaker Gus Andrew Anderson Dies at 86." *Wine Spectator,* December 6, 2016. https://www.winespectator.com/articles/gus-andrew-anderson-dies.

Yahoo Finance. "Vanguard 500 Index Fund Investor Shares." 2008 Performance. Accessed August 31, 2020. https://finance.yahoo.com/quote/vfinx/performance/.

Zwieg, Jason. "How May Day Remade Wall Street." *A Safe Haven for Investors* (blog), May 1, 2015. https://jasonzweig.com/how-may-day-remade-wall-street/.

Chapter 8

Aldred, John. "The World's First Digital Camera, Introduced by the Man Who Invented It." *DIY*

Photography, August 2, 2016. https://www.diyphotography. net/worlds-first-digital-camera-introduced-man-invented/.

Amadeo, Kimberly, and Somer G. Andeson. "Unemployment Rate by Year since 1929 Compared to Inflation and GDP: U.S. Unemployment Rate History." *The Balance*, Updated August 7, 2020. https://www.thebalance.com/ unemployment-rate-by-year-3305506.

"Apple: Number of Employees 2006-2020 | AAPL." *Macrotrends*, Accessed April 22, 2020. https://www.macrotrends. net/stocks/charts/AAPL/apple/number-of-employees.

Carrington, David. "How Many Photos Will Be Taken in 2020?" *Inspiration/Tech Today*(blog). *Focus Mylio*, January 10, 2020. https://focus.mylio.com/tech-today/ how-many-photos-will-be-taken-in-2020.

"Consumer Credit Outstanding and Finance Rates, 1980 to 2000." *Infoplease*, Accessed March 25, 2020. https:// www.infoplease.com/business-finance/personal-finance/ consumer-credit-outstanding-and-finance-rates-1980-2000.

"Fortune 500: A Database of 50 Years of Fortune's List of America's Largest Corporations." *Fortune*, Accessed August 31, 2020. https://archive.fortune.com/magazines/fortune/ fortune500_archive/full/1988/.

Grant, Robert. *Contemporary Strategy Analysis*. 8th edition. United Kingdom: John Wiley & Sons Ltd, 2013.

Hudson, Andrew. "The Rise & Fall of Kodak: A Brief History of The Eastman Kodak Company, 1880 to 2012." *Photosecrets*, August 29, 2012. https://www.photosecrets.com/the-rise-and-fall-of-kodak.

"Kodak Reports Full-Year 2019 Financial Results." *AP News*, March 17, 2020. https://apnews.com/Business%20Wire/44081162267c4549ad5d117260d2a68e#:~:text=Eastman%20Kodak%20Company%20(NYSE%3A%20KODK,of%20the%20Flexographic%20Packaging%20Division.

Juma, Calestous. "Resistance is Futile." Interview by Ramtin Arablouei and Rund Abdelfatah. *Throughline*, NPR, April 25, 2019. Audio, 37:01. https://www.npr.org/2019/04/23/716521520/resistance-is-futile.

Weisberger, Bernard. "You Press the Button, We Do the Rest." *American Heritage*, October 1972. https://www.americanheritage.com/you-press-button-we-do-rest.

Wolpin, Stewart. "20 Years Ago, Apple and Kodak Launched the Digital Camera Revolution." *Mashable*, June 21, 2014. https://mashable.com/2014/06/21/digital-camera-20th-anniversary/.

Chapter 9
Beck, Randall J., and Jim Harter. "Why Great Managers Are So Rare." *Gallup Workplace Business Journal*, Accessed June 17, 2020. https://www.gallup.com/workplace/231593/why-great-managers-rare.aspx.

Chamorro-Premuzic, Tomas. *Why Do So Many Incompetent Men Become Leaders?: (And How to Fix It)*. Boston: Harvard Business Review Press, 2019.

Evans, Lisa. "How to Build a Culture of Trust in Your Company." *Fast Company*, December 11, 2018. https://www.fastcompany.com/90275112/how-to-build-a-culture-of-trust-in-your-company.

Great Place to Work. "The Definition of a Great Workplace." Accessed May 8, 2020. https://www.greatplacetowork.com/trust-model.

Harter, Jim. "Why Some Leaders Have Their Employees' Trust, and Some Don't." *Gallup Workplace*, June 13, 2019. https://www.gallup.com/workplace/258197/why-leaders-employees-trust-don.aspx.

Meinert, Dori. "Why Trust Matters at Work: A Culture of Fear Hinders Innovation and Growth." Society for Human Resource Management, May 24, 2018. https://www.shrm.org/hr-today/news/hr-magazine/0618/pages/why-trust-matters-at-work.aspx.

Musilek, Julie. "Why Trust Beats Employee Engagement." (blog). *Great Place to Work*, July 31, 2019. https://www.greatplacetowork.com/resources/blog/why-trust-beats-employee-engagement.

Schwab, Klaus. "The Fourth Industrial Revolution: What It Means, How to Respond." *World Economic Forum*, January 14, 2016. https://www.weforum.org/agenda/2016/01/

the-fourth-industrial-revolution-what-it-means-and-how-to-respond/.

Sorenson, Susan. "How Employees' Strengths Make Your Company Stronger." *Gallup Workplace Business Journal,* Accessed June 12, 2020. https://www.gallup.com/workplace/231605/employees-strengths-company-stronger.aspx.

Southwick, Alison. "Here's How the Motley Fool Landed on INC.'s Best Workplaces List." The Motley Fool. May 8, 2020. https://culture.fool.com/2020/05/heres-how-the-motley-fool-landed-on-inc-s-best-workplaces-list/.

Stubbings, Carol, and Bhushan Sethi. "Talent Trends 2020: Upskilling: Building Confidence in an Uncertain World." *PwC CEO Survey,* Accessed June 15, 2020. https://www.pwc.com/gx/en/ceo-survey/2020/trends/pwc-talent-trends-2020.pdf.

Zak, Paul J. "The Neuroscience of Trust." *Harvard Business Review,* January-February 2017. https://hbr.org/2017/01/the-neuroscience-of-trust.

Zenger, Jack, and Joseph Folkman. "The 3 Elements of Trust." *Harvard Business Review,* February 5, 2019. https://hbr.org/2019/02/the-3-elements-of-trust.

Chapter 10
Horrigan, John B. "Lifelong Learning and Technology." *Pew Research Center,* March 22, 2016. https://www.pewresearch.org/internet/2016/03/22/lifelong-learning-and-technology/.

Hussain, Zarina. "How Lee Kuan Yew Engineered Singapore's Economic Miracle." *BBC News*, March 24, 2015. https://www.bbc.com/news/business-32028693.

Loyd, Sam. *Sam Loyd's Cyclopedia of 5000 Puzzles Tricks and Conundrums: With Answers.* New York: The Lamb Publishing Company, 1914. https://archive.org/details/CyclopediaOfPuzzlesLoyd/page/n191/mode/2up.

Marcus, Pete. "Eight Steps to Becoming a Trusted Advisor." (blog). Harvard - Tech Communications Agency, September 25, 2017. https://www.harvard.co.uk/eight-steps-becoming-trusted-advisor/.

M.J. "How Singapore Gained Its Independence." *The Economist*, March 22, 2015. https://www.economist.com/the-economist-explains/2015/03/22/how-singapore-gained-its-independence.

National Center on Education and The Economy. "Singapore Overview." Accessed May 28, 2020. https://ncee.org/what-we-do/center-on-international-education-benchmarking/top-performing-countries/singapore-overview-2/.

Nations Encyclopedia Online. s.v. "Singapore." Accessed September 15, 2020. https://www.nationsencyclopedia.com/economies/Asia-and-the-Pacific/Singapore.html.

Onink, Troy. "Get $5,250 A Year from Your Employer to Pay For College." *Forbes*, June 30, 2015. https://www.forbes.com/sites/troyonink/2015/06/30/get-5250-a-year-from-your-employer-to-pay-for-college/#4c307221303e.

Tan, Regina. "iGov: The Singapore Model for Online Intersection Between Government and Public." Columbia University New Media and Development Communication, Accessed May 29, 2020. http://www.columbia.edu/itc/sipa/nelson/newmediadev08/Singapore%20-%20Increasing%20Citizens_%20Mindshare%20in%20e-Engagement.html.

The Organization for Economic Co-operation and Development. "Singapore: Rapid Improvement Followed by Strong Performance." 2010. Accessed May 23, 2020. https://www.oecd.org/countries/singapore/46581101.pdf.

United Nations Development Programme. "Human Development Reports." Human Development Index Trends, 1990-2018, table 2. Accessed May 27, 2020. http://hdr.undp.org/en/content/table-2-human-development-index-trends-1990–2018.

Chapter 11

"Amancio Ortega 1936— Biography - Early Career, The Zara Phenomenon, Inditex." Accessed September 18, 2020. https://www.referenceforbusiness.com/biography/M-R/Ortega-Amancio-1936.html.

Beaton, Caroline. "Millennial Duck Syndrome." *Psychology Today*, May 20, 2017. https://www.psychologytoday.com/us/blog/the-gen-y-guide/201705/millennial-duck-syndrome.

Danziger, Pamela N. "Why Zara Succeeds: It Focuses on Pulling People In, Not Pushing Product Out." Forbes. Accessed September 18, 2020. https://www.forbes.com/sites/pamdanziger/2018/04/23/zaras-difference-pull-people-in-not-push-product-out/.

Ferdows, Kasra, Jose A.D. Machuca, and Michael A. Lewis. "ZARA: The World's Largest Fashion Retailer." 2014.

Forbes. "The World's Real-Time Billionaire." Accessed September 18, 2020. https://www.forbes.com/real-time-billionaires/#7be2b5393d78.

Hansen, Suzy. "How Zara Grew into the World's Largest Fashion Retailer." *The New York Times*, November 9, 2012, sec. Magazine. https://www.nytimes.com/2012/11/11/magazine/how-zara-grew-into-the-worlds-largest-fashion-retailer.html.

"Inditex around the World." Inditex.Com. Accessed September 18, 2020. https://www.inditex.com/en/about-us/inditex-around-the-world#continent/000.

Lee, Hau L. "How Extreme Agility Put Zara Ahead in Fast Fashion." December 10, 2019. https://www.ft.com/content/3f581046-cd7c-11e9-b018-ca4456540ea6.

"Our Employees." Inditex.Com. Accessed September 18, 2020. https://www.inditex.com/our-commitment-to-people/our-employees.

Sirkin, Harold L., and George Stalk Jr. "Fix the Process, Not the Problem." *Harvard Business Review*, July-August 1990. https://hbr.org/1990/07/fix-the-process-not-the-problem.

Warren, Katie, and Melissa Wiley. "Meet Amancio Ortega, the Fiercely Private Zara Founder Who's Worth $68.5 Billion and Owns Properties in Madrid, London, and New York City." *Business Insider*, October 29, 2019.

https://www.businessinsider.com/zara-founder-amancio-or-tegas-life-and-houses#:~:text=Ortega%20owns%2059%25%20of%20Inditex,City%2C%20Chicago%2C%20and%20Seattle.

Wigert, Ben, and Sangeeta Agrawal. "Employee Burnout, Part 1: The 5 Main Causes." *Gallup*, July 12, 2018. https://www.gallup.com/workplace/237059/employee-burnout-part-main-causes.aspx.

Made in the USA
Las Vegas, NV
03 November 2023

80183061R00154